THE SERMON
RAN LONG

A MEMOIR OF MARATHONS & MINISTRY

CARL GODWIN & CARLA EWERT

DEDICATION

I dedicate this story of our forty years of ministry to my mom and dad, Roy and Alice Godwin. I will always remember their faithfulness to His cause, without which this story wouldn't be.

I also dedicate it to my other mom and dad, Gayland and Mary Wooldridge. Thank you for raising Gayle as you did—her heart filled with love for Jesus and passion for His cause. Without her there would be no Calvary story.

TABLE OF CONTENTS

AUTHOR'S NOTE

It's unexpected, maybe, to find ministry and marathoning combined in one book, but these two things are my passions. I have devoted the last forty years of my life to building Calvary Community Church in Lincoln, Nebraska. Through prayer and persistence the church that started with five people in a living room is now a vibrant and growing congregation.

Though I had been a convenience runner for years, at the age of fifty-five I discovered the joy of committed distance running and started running marathons. Running has solidified lessons I've learned throughout my life and has revived my passion for life and ministry. It almost feels to me like another vocation. Ministry and marathoning are linked for me in that they are the avenues through which I experience the fullness of God's presence and community with others.

As a pastor, I rely on illustrations and word pictures to help me communicate truths to my congregation. Calvary folk are used to hearing silly stories about my family, dogs, running, and classic cars during sermons.

When I started working on this book, I was frustrated by the fact that telling the events of my life would just touch the surface of what I wanted to say. I wanted to share the lessons and truths I've learned so that maybe you could find something here to help you on your journey. Then it dawned on me that running is full of metaphors for life, and my experiences marathoning connect to my life lessons in surprising ways. I decided to tap into that connection and use running stories to illustrate those lessons.

This book is organized around that idea. Each chapter focuses on a segment of my life. For instance, the first one is about my young years and call to ministry during my teens. Each chapter opens with a running story to illustrate the main lesson I learned in that time of my life. The running stories are not in chronological order though the story of my life is.

Thanks for reading. Whether you're interested in running, ministry, or both, I hope you find something here you can use to inspire and challenge you.

INTRODUCTION

Who would think to look at me, a short, stocky, sixty-something fellow, that I've qualified for the Boston Marathon twice? I came to marathoning late in life and started running with little expectation. I just wanted to run one marathon to cross it off my bucket list, but once I had done one, I was hooked. From there I began to set goals, one of which was qualifying for Boston. For a while that seemed unattainable. Now I can say that the unlikely has happened.

That unexpectedness is, I think, the stuff of life—to see an unlikely possibility in the distance, attach to that possibility, and see it come to pass. The past forty years of ministry at Calvary Community Church have been a series of unlikely accomplishments for my wife, Gayle, and me, most of which can be wholly attributed to two things—persistence and prayer.

I really can't claim any significant talents. I'm an ordinary guy. I'm not gifted or especially intelligent, but I don't quit. Though, like anything, tenacity has its downside. You could call it stubbornness and you'd be right. I can't imagine where I'd be without my counterbalance, my wife, Gayle. Her gentle though insistent faith keeps me grounded. She also seems to have a direct line to Heaven. When she prays, Heaven moves.

It seems to me that when persistence and prayer meet you end up with faith. Hebrews 11:1 says, "Now faith is the substance of things hoped for, the evidence of things not seen."[1] In life we have glimpses of good, moments of inspiration and hope, but then by mile twenty, inspiration is slipping away and hope is buried in pain. We feel like fools for believing anything good. And maybe persistence alone is foolishness. Holding onto something that has no substance is delusion, really, but when we pray, we literally give substance to even unlikely possibilities. With prayer, persistence becomes faith and what was unsubstantial becomes substance—reality. We aren't chasing a moving finish line. It's there, and we'll reach it. Faith says so. Pain and fatigue won't have the final word. There will be victory.

When I think back on the past forty years, I see how unlikely our path has been. From the time we met with three other people in my parents' living room, our hearts filled with dreams of building a church, to now, Gayle and I have over and over again been up against seemingly insurmountable odds. To be honest, I've wanted to quit more than once. Some of the costs of ministry seem, by earthly standards, too high. There has been incredible pain. Sometimes I've been discouraged by my own weakness. I've been shocked by betrayal and loneliness. But through all that, I have seen God do remarkable things. I've seen lives literally changed. I've seen improbable answers to prayer. I can honestly say that I wouldn't choose to do anything else, given another chance.

Life is, no matter how you look at it, a race of endurance. Like a marathon, there will be times of great pain. It is up to us to keep going through those times, and with prayer and purpose our endurance gains meaning. It isn't endurance for the sake of endurance. It is moving toward something. It's a race. You hurt so you can be a part of it and feel the elation at the finish line for having run at all.

This book is a compilation of stories from our forty years of ministry at Calvary Community Church. I share them with you to demonstrate how persistence and prayer have proven God's power to give substance to mere possibility when we act in faith. During these years, we have both endured and rejoiced. We've not yet reached the finish. We're still serving and running our race with endurance so that those we serve can better run theirs.

These stories are mere highlights. There are many more of answered prayer and changed lives that could have been told but not enough pages to hold them all. God has definitely divided the sea that we could walk through on dry land. He has made a way, time and again, through overwhelming obstacles.

LEARNING PERSISTENCE:
MY EARLY YEARS | 1947–1965

1948 | back: Roy and Alice, Alma and Carl Kinzler (Carl holding namesake Carl)
front: Marlene, Mary, Martha

1

ALL IT TAKES IS ALL YOU GOT

–Marc Davis[1]

KANSAS CITY, MISSOURI, November 2, 2002. Race morning was gray and cold. I stood in the crowd of runners anxiously awaiting the start of my first marathon. The runners around me chattered and cheered. They seemed relaxed and excited, but I was nervous, thinking about the miles ahead. Finally, the gun went off. We were on our way.

I had read *The Non-Runner's Marathon Trainer*[2] when I was fifty-four. I didn't know the first thing about distance running. I had been a convenience runner most of my life but had never committed the time and effort it would take to compete in distance races. I got halfway through the book, closed it, laid it on my desk, and said,

"I'm gonna do that. I'm gonna run a marathon before I die."

At age fifty-five, I decided it was time. I pulled out *The Non-Runner's Marathon Trainer* and my planner. The book laid out a week-by-week, four-month training plan for a first marathon. It suggested one long run a week. It said to increase distance by just ten percent a week, no more than that or you'd risk injury. Steady, gradual progress was the key. The training schedule looked like a bell curve. It worked up to a peak and then tapered off again to allow the body to rest a bit before the race. I really liked the clarity of the plan because a goal without a plan is just a wish.

When I started my training, I needed a specific goal to work toward, so I registered for the Kansas City Marathon. I knew nothing about picking a race, but Kansas City wasn't far away, and I could stay with my sister Marlene and her husband, John, who live there. In my planner, I outlined my running schedule. I followed it meticulously over the next four months, and before I knew it, I was running further than I'd ever imaged I could.

I wasn't far into the race when I realized there are a lot of hills in Kansas City, including the well-known Hospital Hill, which seems to be blocks long. I call it well-known, and now I know that it is an infamous part of the Kansas City Marathon. At the time, I was green and knew nothing about the course I was running, aside from what Gayle and I had discovered driving it the previous day. I certainly didn't check out the elevation map as I selected this marathon. Lesson learned.

At mile eight I saw my family on the corner all bundled up. I was just the opposite, generating a lot of heat. I saw them again at fourteen and looked forward to seeing them at twenty, as we had planned the night before. Time seemed to drag from fourteen to twenty. The temperature dropped. The sweat felt cold against me. I was working my way to twenty, feeling cold and exhausted. My legs were beginning to ache and protest. I needed the distraction and encouragement of familiar faces in the crowd. Then I noticed Gayle and the kids ahead just a few blocks. I grabbed gloves from them as I ran by but kept moving.

As I passed the twenty-mile marker, I realized this was a personal record (PR). I had never run more than twenty miles before. *The Non-runner's Marathon Trainer* had me peak at twenty, and I had only run that far once. This was uncharted territory.

After mile twenty the work was excruciating. Picking my feet up and putting them down was increasingly difficult. My legs began to scream at me, and I felt the agony of the latter miles of a marathon. The pain was almost beyond words. I was pushing my body to extremes it had never experienced before. The only thing that would get me to the finish was stubborn persistence.

In those last miles with the pain setting in, I made myself two promises. One, I will finish! I will finish if I have to crawl across that finish line. I know my family is waiting at the end, and I won't let them down. These last miles are mine to do. I will finish. The second promise was, I will never be so crazy as to do this again! I will finish this race, be glad I did a marathon, and NEVER do this again. I vowed that if I could just finish these miles and stop this pain, that would be it for me.

The miles were going by twenty-two, twenty-three, twenty-four. There was never a question in my mind that I would finish, but I wasn't sure how I was going to be able to cope with the pain in my legs and keep going. I just kept moving, promising myself I would never do it again.

When I had reached the last mile, somebody hollered to me, "Less than a mile to go!" Much of the final mile was uphill. I thought it would kill me. I couldn't believe how steep it was, but I put my head down and kept plowing until, finally, I could see the finish ahead. Adrenaline rushed through me. I was actually about to finish. I was going to complete a marathon. Then I could see my family in the cheering crowd.

As I crossed the finish line, everyone was cheering, and I was overcome with feeling. It was elation and relief and pride and humility all mixed. That finish-line-feeling was more intense than I could have anticipated. Since then, I have seen many people finish a marathon and literally cry for joy. There were tears of joy for me too.

Dick Beardsley said, "I've won every race I've ever run,"[3] and I know what he meant. The feeling of having accomplished a task as challenging as a marathon is that of victory regardless of your place in the race. To run that far you have to find a way to conquer pain and pessimism and keep moving. How exhilarating to cross the finish line of my first marathon and know that I had given my all to get there.

As I was pounding out that last mile, promising myself it would be my last marathon mile ever, I couldn't have known it was the beginning a whole new lifestyle instead. A lifestyle with rites of passage that include chaffing, black toenails, dehydration, cramps, and blisters. A lifestyle that would revolve around the joy of running. Though it took a few weeks to get over the physical pain and get back to running, running marathons soon became a norm. Each year I would increase my running. Ten years later, in 2012, my sixty-fifth year, I would log over 1,800 miles and would have completed twenty marathons in the decade between fifty-five and sixty-five. Running would become for me like John A. Kelley said, "A way of life…just like brushing my teeth."[4] I found that marathoning was perfectly suited to my particular strengths and neuroses. I may lack some gifts and talents but I can persist.

I'm not sure where that persistence in me came from—that drive that says, once I've started, I won't quit no matter how badly I want to. Is it born in or simply a matter of discipline? I suppose it's kind of a chicken and egg question. Does discipline come from persistence or does persistence come from discipline? I'd be tempted to say that the answer is yes—all of the above. I can certainly say that I have an innate stubborn will, and over the years, I have learned how discipline can turn will into accomplishment. But I haven't always persisted. In fact, I wonder sometimes if persistence was embarrassed into me a long time ago when a high school football coach called me a quitter.

Growing up in Nebraska meant football was *the* sport. When I was in grade school, the University of Nebraska gave "knothole tickets" to school aged kids to attend the Nebraska football games. It was their way of trying to fill the stadium. With those tickets, we could get into the games for $.50 and sit in the bleachers in the end zone. My friends and I went to all the games. At one game each year, however, our "knothole tickets" were not accepted. On Band Day the high school bands would perform at half time. During the game, they were seated on the bleachers in the end zone—our seats. Well, my buddy Bob and I thought it was our God-given right to go to the Husker games, so we would climb the fence and get in anyway. We were born and raised Husker fans.

I went to Lincoln High, which was the largest high school in the state of Nebraska. There were more than 900 kids in my graduating class. When I got to high school, I wanted to play football. I wanted to play because I was a Nebraskan and had been raised on Husker football, but I also wanted to play football because my dad had played at Gothenburg High School in western Nebraska. He was all-conference and an outstanding center and linebacker. My dad was big, weighed over 200 pounds. But my mom was petite, and I took after my mom.

Carl, 1965, Lincoln High

In spite of my small stature and the stiff competition for spots on the team at our large school, I tried to play football. My junior year it became clear to me that I wasn't going to get on the field much. I tell people I played tailback; every time I got up, coach said, "Get your tail back on the bench." One day I gave it up. I just didn't go to practice. I didn't go to talk to the coach. I didn't go check in my gear or anything. I just quit.

A few days later, I was walking down the hall of our high school. I looked up and right in front of me coming down the hall was football Coach Aldi Johnson. There was nowhere to go. I was caught. He backed me up against the lockers, shook his finger in my face, and used the word 'quit' at least a dozen times. He said, "You quit on your team. You quit on your coach. Is this what you're gonna do in life? Are you just gonna quit when things don't go your way?"

When he left, I was one angry fella, mainly because I knew he was right—there was no excuse for what I had done, but I also knew in that moment that I wasn't a quitter. He may have been right about my decision to quit the team, but he wasn't right about me. I was determined to show him just how wrong he'd been.

When winter sports began, I went out for wrestling as I had previously. This was my sport, and I really wanted to letter. I needed to prove to myself that Coach Johnson was wrong about me, so I gave all I had. There were two guys on the wrestling team I admired: Kenny and Mike. Mike was state champion. Kenny was runner-up for state. I knew if I worked with them, I could do well. I also knew they were the hardest workers on the team and that I would have to be too.

We used to meet down at the University of Nebraska in the old Coliseum every morning at 5:30 and run the halls for four miles. Our philosophy was to outwork our opponents. We believed when you stepped on the mat and looked that guy in the eye, you had to believe in your heart you deserved to win because you had worked harder than he had. With that philosophy and the camaraderie of those two guys, I had a great junior year wrestling at 127 pounds. Then my senior year I wrestled at 138 pounds. I was cutting a lot pounds to weigh in at 138; I weighed in the 150s.

Wrestling became my obsession—getting up at five o'clock every morning, driving to the university, putting down four miles, and then sitting in the cafeteria at lunch time smelling the cinnamon roles, but instead of having lunch, having an orange and a cup of hot tea with a little honey in it. That was what we ate to make weight so that we could win our matches on Friday night. All that work paid off, and I made the state tournament my senior year.

I learned a lot from that experience. I learned how to push myself toward a goal. Even quitting football taught me something about myself. It taught me to face up to my weaknesses, own them, then find a way to excel in my strengths. That moment with Coach Johnson made me look hard at myself. When I did that, I knew I wasn't a quitter. I knew I could work as hard as anyone, and I determined to do it.

High school sports are one thing; a life's work is another, but I've found that the determination not to quit on a goal that feels right in my gut applies on all levels. During my junior year, as I was working so hard at wrestling and learning the importance of endurance and persistence, something very unusual happened to me.

It was my custom to kneel by my bed every night and pray. Instead for several weeks of my junior year, I would just dive in and pull the covers over my head, because I knew what God wanted. God was making it very clear to me He wanted me to be a pastor. There was no question that it was a call from God. John 10:4 says, "[His] sheep follow him because they know his voice."[5] That calling was a pull in my heart, a constant nagging feeling. I knew it was God's voice, and my job was to follow.

I was terrified—not because I didn't want to. Oh, I wanted to, but I was scared to death. I knew I wasn't a good student. For me high school was all about wrestling, dating, and cruisin' around in my peacock blue 1946 Ford—just having fun. I knew that some things would have to change. Besides the immediate changes, I remember thinking if I was a pastor I would have to get up and talk every Sunday. I was sure I wouldn't know what to say. I just figured God had the wrong number.

Despite my fear, I believed that God answers prayer. My parents frequently talked about how God had provided for them through answers to prayer during the Depression and World War II. I often heard these stories on Sunday nights. We used to love to have people over after church for sandwiches and ice cream. If our guests had kids, we would go play. If there weren't kids to play with, I would sit at the table and listen to the adults talk. They would share about how God worked in their lives and answered prayers from years ago. I loved to hear those stories. I grew up with this unshakable confidence that we serve a God who hears and answers prayer.

That confidence in prayer gave me the courage to say yes to God. I was sure this calling was far beyond my abilities, but I knew that if it was what He wanted, He would go before me and see it through.

One night at church we had a guest speaker—must have been a revival service or something. I don't even remember what he preached on, but during the invitation, I felt God say to me very clearly, "You just give me your life, and I'll use it." As the invitational song played, I stood there holding onto the back of the pew in front of me, scared to death to let go and walk down the aisle, but eventually, I slipped out and knelt at the front and said, "Okay, God, I'm yours."

There was a sharing time after the closing prayer, and I stood and said, "God has called me into the ministry." I think people pretty much thought, *Oh my, him?* I don't know that anybody was very excited, but I did make a real choice to surrender to God.

No one was excited except, perhaps, my parents, especially my mom, Alice. My mom's story could be a book of its own, but for now it's enough to tell that her parents homesteaded 160 acres just west of Casper, in Powder River, Wyoming. Mom and her mother lived in a little wooden shanty. Though we don't know for sure what happened, in 1924 her mother was committed to the state hospital in Wyoming, and my mother, at the age of three, was put into the orphanage in Cheyenne.

We're not sure how long Mom was in the orphanage, but she was eventually adopted by a family who didn't really love her. They took her in to get money from the state, and they were unkind to her. When Mom was in her early teens, they moved to Nebraska and lived near a church. One Sunday Mom walked down the street and went to church. When she talked about it years later, she said that was the first time in her life she heard somebody loved her. She not only heard that Jesus loved her, she saw the love of Jesus in Pastor Carl Kinzler, my namesake, and his wife, Alma.

As God would have it, she had gone to a church whose pastor and wife had no children, and they took a great liking to her. When the situation with Mom's adopted family escalated, the Kinzlers went to court and asked if they could have custody of her. The judge gave them custody, and Mom moved to the parsonage for her latter teen years.

The Kinzlers made an indelible mark on her life. I still remember her telling about how she would hear them praying at night. They were very godly people and were loving and kind to my mother. A preacher and his wife changed her life; therefore, all Mom's heroes were preachers. You've heard the Willie Nelson song "My Heroes Have Always Been Cowboys"? Well, my mother's heroes were preachers.

I can remember as a boy coming in the house, and Mom would be listening to the radio as she worked in the kitchen. She always had a Christian station on with a preacher preaching away. In fact, I remember one preacher from down in Corpus Christi, Texas. He would preach, and then he'd take off and start singing. I remember thinking, *Who is this hick you're listening to, Mom?* His name was Lester Roloff. Little did I realize as a boy that one day when I was in ministry and in need of encouragement, Lester Roloff would reach out to me.

My dad was a plumber. I was a PK, not a preacher's kid but a plumber's kid. Dad worked hard as a plumber and became the chief plumbing inspector for the city before he retired. He had served in the Merchant Marines in World War II. He was the cook on the ship and could make a batch of stew to feed 200. We always had

(l to r) in lovely plaid – Mary, Martha, Marlene with little brother Carl

more stew than we knew what to do with on family holidays.

I was the youngest of four and had three older sisters. The oldest was Martha. Then came the twins, Mary and Marlene, and then me, the baby. Mom and Dad made sure our family life revolved around the church. We went to church every Sunday: Sunday school, church, Sunday night church, and then Wednesday night church. If there was a week or two of revival, we were there every night. Mom and Dad believed if the doors of the church were open we should be there.

My parents were committed to my spiritual growth, but it wasn't just their influence that determined my path as a preacher. They never pushed me toward the ministry. In fact, I remember only one time talking about it with my mother. We were riding in the car. Somehow we started talking about my future. She was driving and said something like, "Well, maybe the Lord would call you to be a pastor." The way she said it implied that if He did, I shouldn't stoop to be the President.

We were committed to our little Nazarene church. It never grew past 125 people. It seemed like we had a new pastor every two or three years—Pastor Fischer, Pastor White, Pastor Mowry, Pastor Hizer, Pastor Laws. Yet, I remember riding home after church with my three sisters in the backseat of the car listening to Mom and Dad in the front seat as they talked about the wonderful message. They never complained about a pastor. I'm sure, in all those pastors, we had to have had a loo loo at some point, but they never complained. They were always supportive.

I am grateful to this day for that church. It was through that church, which was committed to preaching the Bible, that I came to know Jesus Christ. There was, however, a constant struggle between the pulpit and pew. The relationship that should be one of the sweetest this side of Heaven, between shepherd and flock, pastor and people, was instead a constant struggle. The people wouldn't give the reins of the church to the pastor because they knew he wasn't going to be there long, and so the pastor, the God-called shepherd, was as frustrated as a termite in a yo-yo because he couldn't lead the church. The old saying is so true, "Everything rises and falls on leadership." The church was confused about who should lead. It wasn't structured for growth and never really did grow. Nevertheless, the Bible was taught, and my parents made sure we were there to hear it.

I didn't always want to go to church. We kids were often bored. There were no children's programs so kids sat in church with their parents. In fact, they said my mom kept the trees around the church trimmed switching me. She would take me out of the service, give me a wailing, and then bring me back in. I had a hard time sitting through church.

Just down the street from our house was a ball field. Often on Sunday afternoons we'd be playing baseball, and Dad would drive up to the field and honk. It didn't matter if I was up to bat, pitching, or on base; when he honked, I had to get in the car. I can still remember the sneers and comments of some of the boys, "He's going to church." I'd get in the backseat and throw my glove between my feet, but I didn't dare say anything, because I didn't have a vote. Dad said I was going to church and I was going.

But, you know, God honored my dad's commitment. At a Wednesday night service when I was nine years old, an older man stood and shared his testimony. He said, "I finished reading the Bible through the this year." He told us how the Bible had been a blessing to him. I thought, *Wow, that's incredible. He read the whole book.*

I asked for a Bible for Christmas. I got one with my name on the front and a zipper around it. I wrote my name and "From Mom and Dad, for Christmas, 1956," on the page in the front. I still keep that Bible in the drawer by my bed. The binding is broken, but it's all there.

I started reading a chapter a night before I went to bed. Nobody told me where to start. I just thought you started with page one. I started in Genesis, and I read through the Pentateuch, the books of Moses. Then I read the historical books. I read about Jehosaphat and the fat Fellows, Jeroboam and Rehoboam and the Boam boys, all the judges, kings, and prophets.

I noticed that God would summarize a man's life in one verse: so-and-so was a wicked king and departed from the ways of God, died and was buried with his fathers, or so and so was a godly king and walked with God all the days of his life. I remember as a boy saying to myself, "When I die, they're gonna say, 'He lived for God.'" I didn't know then that God wanted me to be a pastor, but I remember as a boy determining to live for God.

Just as I was learning that dogged persistence would get me through and developing one of my life mottos, "I'm in it for the long-haul," I made the commitment to serve God as a pastor. I knew that it was a commitment for a lifetime.

REALIZING POTENTIAL
THROUGH CAMARADERIE:
COLLEGE DAYS | 1965–1970

May 16, 1970 | Carl & Gayle
Guymon, Oklahoma

2

HELP IN TIME OF NEED
—Hebrews 4:16[1]

TRAVERSE CITY, MICHIGAN, May 26, 2007. A million things can go wrong in any marathon. Stakes are high when you commit to a race and spend months training. You want everything to go right, and it usually doesn't. But now and then, a race comes together perfectly. For me, that race was the 2007 Bayshore Marathon, my tenth marathon, when, due to some unexpected and well-timed help, I achieved my first sub-four—I ran a marathon in less than four hours.

Traverse City, Michigan, is a stately, old town. Gayle and I walked the historic streets and shopped the day before the race. That night my left leg ached. I was concerned I had over-trained. I wondered how I was a going to run 26.2 miles if a little bit of shopping made me achy. Of course, I'd rather run a marathon than shop, so maybe my legs would better endure the race.

The day of the marathon was beautiful. The sky was clear, and the air was crisp but not cold. Gayle dropped me off at the start. Waiting for the race to begin, the runners were in high spirits. Race day is always a celebration. Runners run a lot of lonely miles and train for months for the chance to compete. The race is the fun part, the reward, and the beginning of the race is always upbeat as runners connect and enjoy each other's company.

The race was about to start, and I didn't know anyone. I didn't have a running partner, which usually doesn't bother me. I run solo a lot, just me and my dog Scout, but even Scout wasn't there, and I felt a bit low as I watched the jubilation around me. Everyone else seemed to have connections. I prayed, "I could use a friend to talk to in this race."

The starting gun went off, and we were on our way. The course wound through the avenues of Traverse City and then out onto the road, going north on the peninsula on Lake Michigan. The sun rose over the water. Elegant homes lined the lake to our left. The first few miles were going well. I felt good.

Around mile four, I noticed there was a tall fellow running next to me. We seemed to be keeping pace stride by stride next to each other. He commented to me about the scenic course. I said, "Yes, we don't have this kind of beauty where I come from."

"Where are you from?" he asked.

"Lincoln, Nebraska. How 'bout you?"

"Dallas, Texas."

"Oh, I have a daughter who lives in McKinney," I told him.

"McKinney, that's where I live."

"Really? What do you do?"

He said, "I'm the host on the Dr. Cooper radio program."
Well, that floored me. "No way!" I said. "I listen to you every week."

Every Sunday on my way home from church, I faithfully listen to the Dr. Cooper fitness program. Dr. Cooper is the father of the fitness movement and wrote the book on aerobics that got America off the couch many years ago. He said exercise deficiency is the most prevalent cause of ill health in America and is a self-inflicted disease.

Turned out, Todd was the host of the show and here I was running beside him. We talked about our families and our work. I shared with him that I'm a pastor and that I was going to be sixty years old in two weeks. He told me he was going to mention me on the next show.

Around mile fifteen we ran through an aid station. My routine was to grab a cup of water, crease the cup into a V, and slosh it down while I ran. Todd stopped and walked through the aid stations and then caught up with me, but at this one, I lost him. We didn't connect again, so I ran solo for a while but was thankful that God answered my prayer and gave me a friend to run with for so long.

I saw Gayle at miles six and fifteen. I was keeping a good pace, right at nine-minute miles. At mile twenty-one, I saw Gayle again, and she handed me a peeled orange. She knows I like a cool, juicy orange, because at this point in a race I'm generating a lot of heat, and an orange seems to sit pretty well with me over the last miles.

The night before the race when we were out shopping, I bought Gayle a pink sweatshirt. She bundles up for races, because they start early in the morning, and it's often cool. As I ran, I kept telling myself to look for the pretty girl in pink. I could spot her from a block away. I was reminded as I ran those miles that not only had God answered my prayer and given me a running friend for the day, but many years ago in answer to another prayer, he had given me a friend for life.

Gayle and I have been married for more than forty years. We've had our struggles at times, but we have been a team. In the early years of our marriage, she gave me a card. On the front the little cartoon character said, "It's you and me against the world." The inside said, "Do you think they've got a chance?" That has been our attitude. We're a winning team, her and me and God. We've tried to center our life on the Lord, which helps keep perspective, but it still takes a boatload of commitment to make a marriage. To me commitment is the attitude that we're always going to work it out. We've had our conflicts, but neither of us has ever threatened divorce.

I think Jesus implied that we become a team when we become husband and wife when he said in reference to marriage, "Do not be unequally yoked together."[2] You put a yoke on oxen to go out and plow. A yoke is a tool for work. There is a lot of work to be done in life, and God seems to tell us that husband and wife are a team pulling together. We can get wrapped up in the idea that the marital relationship is all about emotion. Emotion is a wonderful part of marriage, but it's not the only part. Spouses ought to lighten each other's loads and make life easier to shoulder.

Knowing that she's my teammate is why it's so encouraging to look for the pretty girl in pink. She comes to every race. She is an integral part of my strategy. The day before a marathon, we drive the running route to get a feel for it. Often on race day, roads near the course are closed completely, which can make getting around tough, so she likes to drive on our pre-run planning session to spot landmarks to help her navigate. She is not known for her keen sense of direction, so this planning is an important part of our strategy. During our drive, we discuss which mile markers will be easiest to get to and decide if I will shed a long-sleeved layer and hand it to her at, say, mile six, or if she will hand me a drink or energy snack at mile ten, etc. She has never missed our designated meetings, except at the Chicago Marathon, where the only way to reach the mile markers is to battle race day crowds to get on the El.

I think by the end of marathon days, she's about as exhausted as I am. The day starts around 3:00 A.M. I tend to be an early riser so it works for me, but she's a night owl and would just as soon never experience such an early hour. While I'm up having breakfast so my body has time to turn the food into energy before the run, she utters a sentence or two from the bed every now and then to let me know she's "supportive." Then she pulls herself out of bed to help with final preparations, which are few because we do pretty much everything the night before. The bib with my number is already pinned on my shirt and everything is laid out. We double-check our preparations. Then we review where we'll meet and what we need to exchange at each meeting.

When Gayle handed me the orange at mile twenty-one of the Bayshore, I told her I was doing well. If I could keep it up, I would have my best finish yet. I ran on, knowing I had five miles to go and wondering if I could keep my pace at nine minutes a mile. That was a huge if. I had been here before and hadn't been able to keep pace.

As I ran along just past mile twenty-one, I noticed a woman running next to me. We kept pace for at least a mile but never said anything. As we crossed mile twenty-two, I gave our mile time. She didn't say anything, and I wondered if she spoke at all. I think she was just wise and was saving every ounce of energy. After a while, I said to her, "You know, we're on a pace to finish at sub-four." She didn't say anything again. So I said, "I've never done that before."

Finally, she spoke, "You're gonna today." She was keeping a solid pace—right at nine-minute miles when we crossed into mile twenty-three, working our way to twenty-four.

I asked, "How many marathons have you done?"

"This is number forty-one."

Well, that begged the question of her age. My mama didn't have any dumb babies, so I didn't ask that. But I did ask, "When did you start running marathons?"

"When I was twenty-eight."

I did a little calculating in my mind. Two a year, let's say, she had to be nearly fifty years old and I was struggling to keep her pace. I told myself I was going to stay with her no matter what. I had never before been able to sustain nine-minute miles. After mile twenty-four, we were right there at 9:05.

When we got to mile twenty-five, she said, "Just one mile to go."

Nobody was cutting up anymore. Nobody was chitchatting. People were laboring and working. Just one mile to go.

We made our way back into Traverse City, and wouldn't you know it, we came to a hill. It wasn't steep but rose at quite an incline for at least a block. She kept pace, made it right up the hill, and left me behind. My legs were screaming and begging me to stop and here I was facing a hill. When we crested the hill, she was eight paces ahead of me. I told myself I had to catch her. I did my best to pick up speed, and little by little I was gaining. I was six paces behind with a half-mile to mile twenty-six. I just kept working all the way. Finally, I was right behind her, and I said, "I'm still with you."

There it was up ahead. Mile marker twenty-six was a welcome

sight. We made our way from mile twenty-six into the stadium to the finish. People were in the stands cheering, and I realized that I was finishing the best marathon I'd ever run. The adrenaline began to flow. She and I ran side by side around the track. As we came around the last corner, the finish was in front of us. I could see the clock. We crossed the finish line together with a time of chip 3:54:54. Finally, I got that elusive sub-four I had been trying for for so long. I thanked her for helping me get my best time ever. She thanked me for encouraging her in the last miles. We both walked away into the crowd of runners, and I never saw her again.

I saw a line of runners and wondered what was up. Then I realized they were waiting for ice cream. At the start, race officials told us they would have free ice cream at the finish. I got in line. Ice cream is my weakness, and I couldn't think of any thing better in that moment. I was working my way up the line, when my stomach churned. I knew I was going to be sick, but I wasn't about to get out of that line. I wanted ice cream. I closed my mouth tightly, determined to stay in line. When I got to the table, the volunteer asked if I wanted vanilla or chocolate. Well, I couldn't open my mouth or I'd lose it, so I forced a smile, and through closed teeth, I grunted, "Banilla."

I went over and sat on the grassy bank, leaned over, got sick, and then ate my ice cream. After I finished, I left the runners' corral, and there was Gayle. I gave her a sweaty hug and showed her my beautiful medal. We were thrilled about my best time ever. As we walked to the car, it was such a sweet feeling to know that after years of trying, I had accomplished a sub-four, averaging 8:58 per mile.

Proverbs 13:19 says, "Desire realized is sweet to the soul."[3] The ice cream at the end of that race seemed almost symbolic to me. I didn't expect a PR that day. I didn't expect a sub-four. But I had tried for both of those things in every race and to have accomplished both was sweet.

It is funny how you hit a stride and things come together every now and again. It isn't often life works that way, but when it does, it's sweet. Often unanticipated help makes those moments possible. For me in this race, help met me at just the right time. I didn't plan to run with anyone and yet people came along when I needed them.

In my life, I've seen this happen again and again. I start out on what I expect to be solo challenge, and lo and behold, just when I need it, someone is there to help. As far back as Mike and Kenny on the wrestling team, people have come along side me to spur me on and challenge me.

Answering the call to preach was terrifying, partly because it meant I had to go to college. I hadn't really prepared for college. I hadn't laid the groundwork in high school. My studies had not been my priority, and I wasn't sure I could make the grade. I knew I was up against a significant challenge and wasn't sure how God would help me through. But none of this caught God off guard. Again and again through my college years, He provided people to show me possibilities and potential I hadn't recognized.

These people kept me accountable and taught me. They were good friends, who could see my potential better than I could. They showed me possibilities through their own accomplishments and unique gifts. Because of their influence, I accomplished more in my college years than I ever thought possible.

I planned to attend Bethany Nazarene College in Bethany, Oklahoma, which is a suburb of Oklahoma City. All three of my sisters had gone there, and I had been to visit numerous times. I started praying about college, because I was apprehensive. I knew I was going to have to get serious about academics. I had no previous success in that area to build on.

What I needed was a team. I needed camaraderie—people to inspire me and keep me accountable. I didn't know to pray for that at the time, but God seemed to know. Larry Ganshorn, who was four years older than I was and attended our church in Lincoln, asked me if I would be interested in rooming with him that next year at Bethany. I was a little surprised because Larry was going to be a senior while I would be a freshman. I saw some real advantages to it, though, and considered it an answer to prayer.

The freshman dorm was a madhouse—lots of noise all hours of the night. Rooming with Larry, I would be in the upperclassman dorm, which was much nicer. The guys there were serious about academics. I got to know some of the upperclassmen even though I was a freshman. Two of them made a great impression on my life.

One was Jim Dimick. Jim was from Maine. He was an all-state basketball player and played for our college, but his main passion was not basketball. Jim was intense about searching for truth. He was always reading and often read standing up. He would pace back and forth in the room with a book in one hand and a pen in the other so he could make notes. While he walked, he talked about what he was learning. When Jim took a class, he read the textbook in the first week. He had an incredible thirst for knowledge, and his passion was to know scripture.

Another friend who impacted my life was Don Stamps. Don was from Oklahoma City. He ran track and came in second in the mile at the state meet his senior year. Don was a square jaw kind of guy, very lean, without an extra pound on him, and full of energy. He was also an amazing scholar. He knew Greek like the rest of us knew English. In fact, he taught some Greek classes while still a student.

Don and Jim liked to debate doctrine—Calvinism versus Arminianism or whatever the issue. I'd listen and soak it all in. We spent a lot of time at Sam's Donuts down the street from campus. Sam's was open twenty-four hours, so we would go there late at night and get coffee. Oftentimes Don and Jim would get into a debate over some issue. I'm sure if you had heard them, you'd have thought they couldn't stand each other. They would really lock horns. I can still hear Dimick saying to Stamps, "Stamps, you got the brains of a ball bearing," and Stamps would reply, "Dimick, you got the brains of a flea." Back and forth they would go.

We spent a lot of time talking together. Sometimes we would go out to the Canadian River and build a fire and sit and talk until three o'clock in the morning. I learned so much from those guys. Perhaps I learned more Bible from them than I did from my professors.

College life brought new challenges, both academic and financial. I needed to find a job, but my opportunities were limited because I didn't have a car. Eagan Plumbing Company was just two blocks from campus, so I walked over and applied for a job. Since my dad was chief plumbing inspector in Lincoln, I never had any problem getting a job there, but that didn't carry any clout in Oklahoma. I was told they didn't need anyone at Eagan Plumbing.

I didn't have any better luck at other places near campus, and I was becoming desperate. After classes one day, I went to my dorm room, knelt by my bed, and reminded my Heavenly Father of my need. Just then a voice over the intercom said, "There is a man in the lobby who would like to hire someone for a one hour job delivering a hot water heater."

Well, I know when to pray and when to put feet to my prayers. I said, "I'll be right down." In the lobby was Mr. Eagan, owner of

Eagan Plumbing Company. We delivered the hot water heater to the job sight, and as he brought me back to the dorm, he asked if I was still looking for a job.

"Yes, sir," I answered.

"Can you start tomorrow afternoon?"

Thus began a relationship with Eagan Plumbing Company that gave me employment for several years.

At the end of my freshman year, I asked Stamps what I should read that summer. He said to read the life stories of the giants of the faith. I did that while working construction and saving for school. I read the biographies of men like D.L. Moody, Jonathan Goforth, Hudson Taylor, and Billy Sunday. I was inspired by these stories.

That same summer, I reconnected with my high school friend Gary Gregg and found out his mother had had open-heart surgery. Recovering from that kind of surgery was quite an ordeal and required a long stay at the hospital. Well, I saw this as my opportunity to make a pastoral visit. I figured I'd go up and see her. I'd read scripture and pray with her and be a real comfort. I put on a suit and tie and headed to the hospital, Bible in hand.

I wasn't at all prepared for what I would see when I went into her room. She was pale and drawn and had a tracheostomy, which she had to cover to talk. As I tried to talk with her, the room began to spin. I sat down in the chair by her bed, but the room would not stop spinning. Finally, I put my head between my knees, but even that didn't help. I sheepishly told her I'd come back another day. I took no more than three steps out of her room before had to stop and lean against the wall for support. Then I slid down to the floor, nearly passed out.

A nurse came by and wanted to help, but I talked her into letting me recover myself. Then I slipped out of the hospital, berating myself all the way. I hadn't even prayed with Mrs. Gregg. How did I expect to be a pastor if I couldn't make a hospital visit?

I was tormented by my failure. I knew I had to try again. The next week I put on my suit and tie, grabbed my Bible, and went back. This time she was further along in the recovery process, and I was prepared for what I would face. I was determined to do this visit right, so I read some verses and prayed with her. I made it through the entire visit and redeemed my pastoral ambitions.

At the beginning of my sophomore year, Dimick and I were in our bunks talking before we went to sleep. Dimick said, "Carl, what kind of grades are you gonna make this semester?"

I went through my classes one by one and predicted what I thought I could make, "I think I can pull an A in this class, and then in this class I think I can pull a B," as I went through my classes.

When I was finished, Dimick said, "Carl, that's honor roll."

I sat up in my bed in the darkness of the room and said, "I have never made honor roll in my life."

He said, "Well, you're going to this semester," and I did. I went on to get an academic scholarship.

By my junior year, having worked hard to adjust to college, I was doing well. That semester I started Greek class, and I sat in the back row with a friend named Ron Williams. Ron Williams was a campus cut up. He had come from Germany all the way to Oklahoma City to our campus. He was a long way from home and his family and was ready to have fun. Ron and I sat on the back row of Greek class. We passed notes and didn't listen very well the first two weeks. Then we got our first test back. I got 44%, and Ron got 42%—both of us big fat Fs.

We walked out of class, and Ron said, "I'm heading straight over to the administrative building and dropping Greek. We have got to quit this class."

Boy, when Ron said we needed to quit, I remembered Coach Aldi Johnson and heard his railing again and knew I couldn't quit. I said, "No, Ron, I can't quit Greek. It is the language of the New Testament, and I'm preparing for the ministry. I have to learn Greek."

He said, "What are we going to do?"

"Here's the plan, Ron. We're going to get to our next Greek class early and get the front row seat right under the professor's nose, and we are gonna work harder on Greek than all our other classes put together." And that's exactly what we did for the next two years. Ron and I were early everyday and sat on the front row. We worked harder on Greek than we did on all of our other classes combined.

Greek was really hard for me because the professor assumed you knew the ins and outs of the English language, and if you didn't, you could get lost very easily in his lectures. My high school English grades had been less than impressive, so I had to go back and dig up English as well as learn Greek. It was a challenge, but at the end of the two years, I made a 96% on my final and ended up with a B+ in Greek. As important as learning the language of the New Testament was, relearning the rules of English would prove to be just as important in the near future.

The summer after my senior year, I had the opportunity to go to Jasper, Alabama, and work as a youth pastor in a Nazarene church there. There was an influential businessman by the name of Ken Key who made it possible for me to be there that summer. I worked for Ken in his factory and worked in the church as well. John W. Banks was the pastor of the church, and I learned a lot from him that summer.

On Saturday mornings, he was rarely in his office. He didn't mind if I spent time in there studying, so I made a habit of going in on Saturday mornings. I'd go to his desk, sit down in the big leather chair, and get goosebumps, thinking that one-day people would call me pastor. Pastor Banks allowed me to preach several times in his church, and I was able to create a vision of what being a pastor might feel like.

College Graduation, May, 1969

That was a powerful summer in my life. I admired Pastor John W. Banks. I loved his wonderful family. Who wouldn't fall in love with these wonderful "sweet home Alabama" folk? Mrs. Banks could cook, and family meals were an event. I was not only fed fantastic food, my desire to be called pastor was fed, too.

I came back to school after the summer in Jasper, Alabama, to begin my master's program. The first week of school, I was in the cafeteria with a table full of guys. As guys will, we were watching the girls who stood along the wall in the cafeteria line. One of the guys, Ron Wilson—we called him Willie—said to me, "Carl, I met just the girl for you this summer—a freshman girl. Her name's Gayle." Soon she walked by, and Willie pointed her out, "Would you like to meet her?" She was very attractive, and I said of course I would.

A short time later at supper, several guys were sitting around, and Burt Hans was across the table from me. Burt said, "You know, guys, I've got a date with Mary, and I'm really excited about it.

Freshman Gayle Wooldridge

Everything's gotta go right." He told us where they were going and was clearly excited to start the school year right with a date with Mary.

After Burt took his tray and left, I said, "Hey, guys, you know, Burt said he needs to make sure this date goes well. Everything needs to be perfect. Why don't you guys help him out?"

Several guys leaned in, "Sure, how can we do that?"

"Well, he told you where he was going. Why don't you go down there and locate his car and decorate it? Put "just married" on the window and some cans on the back, so when they come out, it will be all decorated. Burt will love it." They took my suggestion, but things like that have a way of coming back to you.

Willie introduced me to Gayle, and I asked her out. I really was impressed with Gayle. Not only was she very lovely, but I could tell after a few conversations that her heart beat for ministry just like mine. After our first date, I went home to my room, knelt by my bed, and said, "God, that's the one I want right there."

On our second date, we doubled for dinner with Willie and his girlfriend. While we were eating, a police officer came up to our table and said, "Does one of you guys own the maroon Oldsmobile in the parking lot?" I thought, *Oh no, somebody hit Willie's car.* The officer grinned and said, "You ought to see it." We knew what it was right then. Burt had taken his revenge. I was concerned what our

43

dates would think. When we went out, that car was decorated as if we'd been to the chapel instead of the local diner. "Just married" was written across the back window. Tin cans were tied to the bumper. Vaseline smeared on the door handles. The girls just laughed.

In those days we had a midnight curfew on weekends, so there was always a midnight rush in front of the girls' dorms as fellows dropped off their dates. We pulled up with that car decorated, and everybody was looking and laughing. The girls didn't mind; they just played up the joke. I loved that Gayle was able to laugh about it. I remember thinking in my heart, *Someday it won't be a joke; it will be the real thing.*

After we had dated for several weeks, I wanted Gayle to meet Jim and Jeanne Lynch. The year before, I had been given a ministry assignment in their little church in Hydro, Oklahoma. Hydro was a one-horse town an hour west of Bethany. The church met in a small, white, frame building. The parsonage was next door. On a good Sunday, we would have forty people in church, maybe fifty on a special day. Most of those good, faithful people would return for Sunday evening services, and Jim often had me preach. That was where I cut my preaching teeth.

What started as simply a ministry assignment became a passion for me. I loved getting off campus, away from the world of academia into the "real world" of ministry. Jim and I could not have hit it off better. Our hearts were knit together as friends and co-workers. He taught me many things.

One Sunday I was in charge of the service. I welcomed people, made announcements, and then turned the pulpit over to Pastor Jim to preach, but I forgot take the offering. He covered for me and took the offering before he brought his message. That afternoon as we enjoyed Sunday dinner together, he said to me, "Carl, forgetting to take the offering is something you won't do when you're pastor." How right he was.

When I started to have serious feelings for Gayle, I felt like I needed to get the Lynchs' approval. Of course, I knew they would love her so maybe I was just showing off. I brought her with me one Sunday morning and introduced her to them and the dear people of the church. After Sunday dinner at the parsonage, Gayle and I walked back over to the little church.

As we walked up the aisle, I told Gayle about the great times I had had ministering there. We went onto the platform and stepped behind the pulpit. We looked out over the empty pews and were quiet, as we sensed the weight of the moment. I looked into her eyes. We knew without saying it that we would have a future together—a future that would revolve around the church, the pulpit, and ministry. We kissed, and as we walked away holding hands, we both felt God's work in our hearts. He was not only giving us a love for each other but also a shared passion for Him and His cause.

I certainly did not know how to propose to her. I knew I wanted to marry her, but I couldn't figure out how to just ask her outright. Later that fall, we were at the lake near my sister's house, walking along watching the ducks. The air was crisp, so we got back in the car to warm up. I wanted to ask her—to pop the question, but I didn't know how. Just then the Supremes came on the radio singing "Someday We'll Be Together." I looked over at Gayle and said quietly, "Someday we'll be together, won't we?" She grinned and said yes and kissed me. After that we went shopping for a ring and set our wedding date.

Two days after school was out for the year, we got married in Gayle's hometown Guymon, Oklahoma, which is five hours from Oklahoma City. I couldn't believe how many kids came that distance. My roommate, Howard Day, was my best man, and Jim Dimick and Willie—Ron Wilson and Burt Hans stood up for me. After the wedding and the reception, Gayle and I changed our clothes and were ready to leave for our honeymoon. When we came out to get in the car,

Carl retrieving his bride at her home following her "kidnapping"

about ten guys grabbed me and held me back and took Gayle. They kidnapped her, put her in a car, and drove off. Eventually, I found out they took her home to her parents' house, and I drove over to get her.

When I got there, I saw a line of cars a couple of blocks long in front of the house. This was 1970, the day of muscle cars, and these guys' cars had some big engines. You could hear them all over town. There were seventeen cars lined up to chase us as we drove out of town. I grabbed Gayle, and we took off, seventeen cars following us.

From time to time, one of them would pull up beside me, and I would gun it. I knew if they got around to make me pull over, they would take my bride again. We were going down the highway heading west out of Guymon toward Colorado, and all of a sudden I saw lights, emergency lights, flashing ahead. I slowed down as a trooper signaled me to pull over. I pulled over to the shoulder, and seventeen cars behind me pulled over. Of course, the officer could see what it was all about because my car was decorated for the occasion.

He said, "Looks like maybe you have a little problem here."

"I do, officer. They already stole my bride once, and I'm just trying to get out of town."

The officer replied, "I'll make a deal with you. If you go the speed limit, I'll hold them all back."

I said, "You got a deal. Thank you, sir."

He held them all back, and I waved goodbye. We headed west and didn't see that bunch again.

My years in college pushed me beyond my imagination academically largely through the influence of fellow students and friends. They urged me on, believed in me, and their encouragement helped me reach potential I never knew I had. I grew in unexpected ways through the influence of people God brought into my life. I could see God providing and answering prayer. It is true that "when God guides, God provides."

Ultimately God provided my life's teammate in Gayle. I had been filled with anticipation and excitement about the dream of one day being called pastor. Now it wasn't just me; it was we. God had given me someone whose heart beat like mine to share the dream.

MORE THAN LIKE-TO:
TRAINING FOR MINISTRY | 1970–1972

Carl and John after a WhistleStop Marathon PR

3

ASHLAND, WISCONSIN, October 15, 2005. Not long after I began running marathons, I talked my brother-in-law John and my nephew Chris into running with me. We ran the North Olympic Marathon together. They caught the marathon bug and began distance running regularly. Before long they were pushing me to get a sub-four. If I could run a marathon in less than four hours, I would Boston Qualify (BQ) in the sixty to sixty-four age bracket.

Qualifying for Boston became my goal. It was a real challenge and that excited me. I had never run a marathon in four hours. I knew it would take loads of commitment and preparation to push this old body to that limit.

Running has taught me again how important preparation is.

It has affected every area of my life. My diet has changed. I have learned to eat a more natural and plant based diet. My schedule has changed. I run for hours each week and have to make sacrifices to do so. My priorities have changed. I don't miss a run—all this preparation in pursuit of a goal.

We tend to want to skip right to the good part—race day, but without prep, race day would mean little. Even if I finished a race I hadn't prepared for, I know it would mean less to me than one that had taken hard work and commitment.

Thankfully, I guess, things have never come easily to me. I'm not an extraordinary person in any way. I'm not terribly charismatic as some pastors are. I am neither incredibly intelligent nor that eloquent as some would expect a pastor to be. As far as running goes, I'm about the furthest thing from what you imagine a runner to be. Now, John, he looks like a runner. He's tall and lanky. He doesn't have an extra ounce on him. His strides cover several feet and look smooth. But me, I'm stocky. I'm short. My strides are clipped and choppy. I don't really look like a marathoner, but I work really hard to be one. I love being one. It's the challenge and the work that make me love it.

One of the great things about running is that it doesn't really matter if you're a John or a Carl. Anyone can run. There's a quote by Maurice Greene that illustrates this for me. He said, "Every morning in Africa a gazelle wakes up. It knows it must move faster than the fastest lion or it will not survive. Every morning a lion wakes up and it knows it must move faster than the slowest gazelle or it will starve. It doesn't matter if you are the lion or the gazelle, when the sun comes up in Africa you better be moving."[1] Whether you're built like a gazelle or a lion, you must move.

But even with prep and discipline, the unexpected happens. After close-but-not-quite times in a couple of marathons, I decided my best shot at Boston was my old stand by, Whistlestop Marathon in Ashland, Wisconsin.

John came to run with me to pace me. We had a great day for the race and were clipping the miles off one after another, talking as we went, enjoying the scenery. The trees that lined the trail were bright yellow and red with fall leaves. The race went smoothly, and our pace was solid when we reached the last 385 yards. A sub-four was within reach.

I could see the finish line. John and I were in the little town of Ashland. People were cheering. We crossed mile twenty-six and were only two blocks away from the finish when I got a major cramp in my left calf. I grabbed John's shoulder to keep from going down. We were in the middle of the street, and it was all I could do to stay on my feet. It took me about a minute to work that cramp out. I finished the last two blocks with a limp and crossed the finish line. To my disappointment, our time was 4:01:44. We missed our goal. I was disappointed because we were shooting for sub-four— that elusive sub-four. Even so, it was the best time I'd ever had—a personal record (PR). What matters more than victory is what we do to reach it. All that prep was victory in itself. It had carried me this far, and I believed it would get me into Boston.

Throughout my life I've relied on discipline to reach my goals. It's easy to see its impact where running is concerned, but discipline matters in all areas of life. Discipline will build character. Character is doing right whether you feel like it or not. Scripture talks a lot about this, because, while one becomes a Christian by grace, spiritual growth involves discipline. This doesn't mean we'll attain everything we work for. There are set backs in life. Real ones. But it does mean that we will be satisfied with ourselves in the process of life.

Paul wrote to young Timothy in I Timothy 4:7, "Discipline yourself for the purpose of godliness."[2] He went on in verses fifteen and sixteen, "Take pains with these things. Be absorbed in them so that your progress will be evident to all. Pay close attention to yourself and to your teaching. Persevere in these things."[3] Wow, "take pains," "be absorbed . . . so your progress will be seen by all." "Pay close attention to your growth." "Persevere." That could be encouragement to a runner.

It's how we live each day that counts. There are days you feel like running and days you don't. Making the decision to run regardless of how you feel is what makes you a runner, and those daily runs add up to a successful race day. Big accomplishments come from small actions. Once you perform an action and you perform it repeatedly, whether it's a good or bad, it becomes a tendency. Before you know it, you're on automatic pilot. Will is hardly involved. First we make our habits, and then our habits make us.

Sometimes people say to me, "I'd like to run a marathon someday." In fact, several people in our congregation have taken up running. They know that it takes more than like-to. It takes commitment and determination. You have to be intentional. Put it on the calendar and commit to following your schedule. Do it whether you feel like it or not. Like-tos must fall by the wayside if we're going to achieve our goals.

The funny thing about preparation is that we often don't know exactly how it's going to pay off. In some cases uncertainty can keep you from wanting to put in the daily work, but persist anyway. You'll find that the daily work will come together in unforeseeable ways to move you closer to your goals.

As I neared the end of my time in college, I began to do things I hoped would prepare me for real ministry. I didn't always know how my work would impact my future ministry. I have been shocked by how God honored even the clumsiest of my efforts at preparing myself. So often those efforts have paid off in unexpected ways.

Gayle and I got married at the very beginning of the summer of 1970 because we had signed on to work with Southwestern Publishing Company that summer. Southwestern was the largest employer of college students in the United States. They sent you door-to-door selling books. They trained you and taught you how to work with people. For me, it was a chance to make good money, but more than that, it was experience learning how to talk to people, which is a great help for ministry.

After the wedding and a honeymoon in Colorado, Gayle and I headed to Nashville for sales training two weeks behind rest of the team from Bethany. I drove a 1967 Mustang at the time, and it was loaded with our stuff. We drove all day. Toward evening, we came over the hill and saw the lights of Nashville all spread out in front of us. I was very impressed. The city looked huge. I had the address of the sales school but no idea how to find it. I looked out over Nashville and then over at the passenger seat and saw my pretty bride. I realized I had a big responsibility, and my only source of income was a one hundred percent commission job selling books. I had $100 in my billfold I'd borrowed from my sister Mary. My team was already two weeks ahead of me. I was overwhelmed and thought a prayer, *Lord, help me.*

About that time on the expressway, a car next to us honked. The guys in the car were waving at us, and I recognized one of them from our college. We all pulled over on the shoulder, and they asked if we were heading to sales school.

"Yes," I said, "and we've never been there before."

They said, "Follow us."

I breathed a prayer of thanks, and relief filled me as we followed them. On the way, we stopped to get some supper. A guy named Darrell sat across from me. I began to ask him questions about Southwestern Publishing Company. He was a pre-med student and had done very well selling books in the past.

When he told me he was coming back for his fifth summer, I asked, "So you've got a good team with you?"

He said, "No, I don't have a team at all. I hadn't planned to come back. I decided to at the last minute because other summer plans fell through."

When we got to sales school, our manager said that Darrell would train me that week. Although I didn't have Alden Laird, my student manager from Bethany who was already on the book field, this was even better. Alden had a team of nineteen students, but I had Darrell all to myself.

Sales students stayed in a downtown hotel and went to classes during the day. After class Darrell and I would work all evening. He taught me how to give my demo. He'd have me knock on the door. I would start my presentation, and he'd slam the door in my face. He would call me at 5:30 in the morning and say, "Hey, if you're gonna have a great summer, you can't be sleeping in."

At the end of the week, Darrell sat Gayle and me down and said, "You know, I've trained a lot of people in sales school, but you have worked harder than anybody I've ever worked with." He said, "You guys will have a great summer." I don't know if he said that just to make us feel good or what, but it worked. We believed it.

From training we went to our book field in Atlanta, Georgia. We located in Decatur, a suburb of Atlanta, and found an inexpensive place. It was a little apartment in a huge, old, southern house shaded by large trees. Two little, old ladies owned it and lived in part of it. The shade trees made that summer in hot Atlanta bearable since the apartment didn't have air-conditioning. Across the street was a train track, but we got used to the noise pretty quickly. It took us a little longer to get used to the big cockroaches. That was our first place together.

I really believed in the books I was selling. It was a set of Bible study books that included a Bible commentary, a Bible encyclopedia, a Bible history book, and Bible storybook for children. I believed everybody in Atlanta ought to have a set, and I sold like it. I would start in the morning and demo and sell those books all day long. We had a great summer. Of 5,000 first-year student salespeople, we finished fourth in the company, though we started a couple weeks later than most of the teams.

Gayle was our accountant. She kept the books, sending every dollar possible to headquarters to reap at summer's end. In fact, she won the "Tough-Minded Businessman Award" because she figured our check to the last penny. When we got back to Nashville at the end of the summer, she was able to tell them exactly what our check should be. It was just over $3,600 for a summer's work, which was a phenomenal amount of money to make in 1970.

After another year of graduate school, we returned to the book field with Southwestern for our second summer. This time we took a team. I recruited ten students and was their student manager. I worked with them through the week of sales school, and then we were sent to Charleston, South Carolina, and the surrounding area.

Several of my guys rode bicycles because they didn't have cars, so I let them have the city of Charleston, and I took a rural area. I sold in a town called Barneville, South Carolina, which is about forty miles west of Charleston. I would meet with my team every Sunday after church for an inspirational meeting to prepare for another six days of selling.

My first two weeks in Barneville were really good, but once I covered the little town, I began selling in the surrounding rural area. Outside of town, it seemed every person I spoke to said, "Boy, I like that set and would like to purchase it, but you see, I just bought this new family Bible." In many cases they would hold it up and show it to me—a nice, big, family Bible produced by our company, Southwestern Publishing. They would say, "I bought this from a kid from Indiana who drives a red Volkswagen and is getting married at the end of the summer." I don't know how many times I heard that. I never came across the kid, but he was from the family Bible division of Southwestern. He was selling the big family Bible, drove a little red Volkswagen, and was getting married at the end of the summer. He had my territory pretty well covered and was beating me to the punch. So for a couple weeks my sales were bad. It was terrible to have recruited ten guys, and though I was their leader, they were almost outselling me. I was supposed to be one of the top sales guys in the company, and I was striking out.

This went on for three weeks. The third week, I kept hearing the same story, "I would sure like to buy that set, but I just bought this family Bible from a young man from Indiana who drives a red Volkswagen and is getting married at the end of the summer." At the end of the week, after hearing that story for the umpteenth time, I went out of the house, set my case down, sat down on the grass in the front yard, and put my head in my hands. That little four-letter word came to my mind: Q U I T. I knew I wouldn't quit. I couldn't quit, but I couldn't go on like that.

I went back to Barneville and told Gayle, "We're moving." This was a no-no in the company. You didn't just up and move without the permission of your sales manager in Nashville, but we packed up and left the little place we had found in Barneville and moved to Charleston. We found a place to live in Charleston, and as quickly as I could, I got back on the circuit and started selling.

Since I needed to leave Charleston to my team, I started selling east of Charleston in the Francis Marion National Forest. My sales turned around right away. I found that people lived all around their relatives. I would sell to the first Gaskin family. Then as I was leaving, I would ask, "Now, who lives in the house down the road?"

They would tell me, "Oh, that's my brother Charlie."

So I would go to Charlie and say, "You know, your brother Orville just bought this set, and he was so excited to get it." Charlie wasn't going to be outdone, so he would buy the set. When I'd leave there I'd say, "Now, let's see, who lives down the road in the next house?"

He'd say, "That's my Uncle Wilbur." On it would go. Some days I'd sell to the same family one member after another most of the day.

The Francis Marion National Forest was rough country. In fact, when I told people in Charleston where I was selling, they would say, "Oh, you're up in Hell Hole. You should be careful." I didn't really think much of it, but I should have. I soon learned how true it was that the gun was the law of the land up there.

The houses were wooden, and sometimes there were gaps in the wall big enough you could throw a cat through. Time and again as I would be making a demo to a lady, she would pick up a coffee can and spit in it. I realized these ladies were chewing tobacco. I had never seen that before, but it was very common out there.

It seemed like I sold to everybody in the Francis Marion National

Forest, and at the end of the summer, it was time to deliver the books. When I was selling, I went by myself and was gone from morning till dark. At delivery time, Gayle went with me to help keep things organized and drive so I could hop out and drop off books.

We learned during training never to leave books without payment—a good rule, I found out. During delivery week sometimes you'd come with the books, and people would say, "Well, I can pay you later this week if you want to just leave the books now." At one house, I left the books on the woman's word that she would have the money Friday. I came back Friday, and she said, "Oh, you know, looks like it'll be Tuesday. Can you come back on Tuesday?" When I came back Tuesday, she wasn't home. This happened several times, and it was a forty-five mile drive from Charleston up to her house. Finally, I caught her at home.

I let her know I was there to collect for the books, and again she asked me to come back next week. I said, "This is my fourth trip, and I need you to pay me." When she told me I'd have to wait until next week, I got up and walked across the room to where the books were on a shelf. I picked them up and walked out of the house. She started yelling, grabbed her pistol, and followed me out. She pointed it at me and pulled the trigger several times. I was shocked, but it just clicked over and over again.

Gayle was behind the wheel, and I said, "Start the car. Let's go." She was so nervous when she saw what was going on she couldn't get the car started. I said, "Scoot over," jumped in, and started the car. As I did, the lady pulled the magazine down out of the little pistol, shoved it back in, pulled the trigger, and, BOOM, it went off. She wasn't standing three feet from me, and it went off. At that same time, her son came out the front door with a shotgun. I reached over with my right hand and pushed Gayle's head down and drove with

Carl pointing to bullet hole in our car

my left hand. We tore down that dirt road in a cloud of dust.

We drove straight to the magistrate—that was the sheriff. I knew where he lived. I had sold him books too. When I got there, I told him what had happened. He said, "Listen, you made a great mistake. You should have come to get me first instead of picking up those books and walking out of her house when she had possession of them. She knew she had the right to shoot you." He said, "We go there all the time and pick up things that those people order and never pay for. They know their rights. You are fortunate to be alive." She had shot a hole right through the driver's door of my car. We found out why Hell Hole was the unofficial name of the beautiful Francis Marion National Forest.

Those summers were hard work. I worked long hours and talked to dozens of new people every day. Though I believed selling books would be good experience for ministry, I had no idea how valuable the simple process of knocking on doors and talking to new people would be to me in later years. I did my daily work and did my best. That commitment would end up benefitting me in ways I couldn't have foreseen.

Back at Bethany that fall, I was in my last year of graduate school and was close to beginning ministry. I began to take a good, hard look at the structure in the Nazarene church. Here's how it looked to me: if you did a good job with a church, you could gain the favor of the district superintendent. Then he would move you to another church. If you did your best there and stayed on the good side of the district superintendent, he'd get you a better church, and you'd keep moving up until you became a district superintendent. The administrative position of district superintendent was a big deal in the denomination.

As I was struggling with all of this, someone said to me, "You know, you'll probably be a district superintendent someday," and it bothered me like fingernails on a chalkboard. In my thinking there was no higher calling than being a pastor. I didn't see all this denominational hierarchy in the New Testament. I did see a lot about being a pastor and qualifications for a pastor.

I knew that Jesus had said, "I will build my church." If you were to ask me, "What is God doing? What is God up to?" I would respond that He's building His church in this world. He said that we are co-laborers with Him. I was excited about being a co-laborer with Him in the greatest cause known to man, building a church.

I wanted to build a church. I didn't want to play politics, but that was all I could see as I remembered my experience of having so many different pastors as I was growing up. We would just begin to get to know and love a pastor, and then he would announce he was moving on. I knew that a change in pastor is to a church what a heart transplant is to the body. It's always traumatic. Sometimes there are difficulties. In some cases even rejection. I thought, *Is this really what I want to give my life to?* It was frustrating because I knew I was called, and yet I found the situation disappointing at best, intolerable at worst.

But churches in America were changing. There was a movement toward independent churches, which made the mega-churches of today possible, for better or worse. Of course, I couldn't see all

*Early married life with
"our baby" Husker*

that at the time, but I did know I wanted something different from what I had known.

One day I was in the bookstore, and I picked up a book by Dr. Elmer Towns, *The Ten Largest Sunday Schools in America* and *What Makes Them Grow.*[4] I didn't know who Dr. Elmer Towns was. I'd never heard of him, and I never dreamed I'd meet the man, but I bought the book and devoured it. I had no idea that book would change the direction of my life.

As I read about these churches, I was moved and inspired by their vision. They wanted to grow and reach people for Christ. I saw that the churches profiled in the book shared some common denominators. One was the average tenure of the pastors, which was over twenty years.

I went to my director of studies and asked him if I could write my thesis on the subject of church growth and do a study of some of these churches. Of course, none of the ten were Nazarene, so the response was, "No, I don't think that would be a contribution to knowledge." It seemed it was too practical. Somebody might take the information and use it.

Nevertheless, I was determined to learn more about this type of church. I told Gayle, "When I finish graduate school, I want to take a year and see these churches first-hand. I want to study them to learn the principles of church growth. Then we'll take a church in our denomination, and we'll make it different." I figured if I had forty years to pastor, I would rather take one year to really prepare and settle for thirty-nine years of productive ministry rather than dive right in not really knowing what I was doing.

I knew that preparation could make or break a plan, but I didn't know that God would use the prep I did in bigger ways than I had planned.

WALK WITH WISE MEN:
FORMING OUR VISION | 1972–1973

Carl and Husker proud of their overhaul

4

LINCOLN, NEBRASKA, September 23, 2006. Reading *Runner's World* magazine, I found out Dean Karnazes, the nationally known ultra distance runner, was doing fifty marathons in fifty states in fifty days and was scheduled to be in Lincoln on September 23. Dean won the 2004 Badwater Ultramarathon in Death Valley, which has been called "the world's toughest race," running 135 miles in 120 degree temperatures in twenty-seven hours and twenty-two minutes—a mind-blowing achievement.

I was scheduled to peak in my training that same Saturday, three weeks before my next race. I could do my peak run with one of the greatest runners in the country. I signed up.

I drove downtown for the run. It was a football game day in Lincoln, and I couldn't find a place to park anywhere since the course started right in front of the stadium. This wouldn't be a live marathon, but it would follow the course for the annual Lincoln Marathon, which runs a loop around the city, returns to the stadium, and ends on the football field. Of course, we would finish in front of the stadium since it was a game day, and we couldn't run onto the field. I finally found a place to park in a parking garage about a mile from the start and did a warm up run back to the start of the marathon. Gotta love Husker fans.

About twenty people were there to run with Dean. We took off at his pace. According to the website, his pace would be a nine and a half minute mile. That was perfect for my training. I try to maintain about nine minute miles on race days, so my training pace is closer to ten-minute miles, but nine and a half was doable.

Running with Dean was a rich experience. He talked all the way and was very friendly. He told stories about some of his running experiences and answered our questions. He told us that he believes running is purest form of athletic expression. He explained his training and diet. He said if you temper your body with pain, it will amaze you, and you will be able to do things you thought impossible.

It was a beautiful day, and Lincoln is primarily flat, so the course was gentle. When we neared Holmes Lake, the Lincoln Marathon organizers, who were leading us on bikes, told us we had crossed mile twenty. A couple of college guys said, "Hey, I smell the barn. Let's pick it up." And they did. The nine and a half minute pace went out the window. My pride got the best of me. I wasn't going to let them leave me behind. I found a higher gear and finished hard. The nine of us who finished with Dean had our picture taken with him.

When you have the opportunity to be around someone who is successful in the field you want to be in, take it. I love what Coach John Wooden said, "It's what you learn after you know it all that counts."[1] We never really know it all. We have to keep learning, and listening is essential to learning. Find someone who knows more than you do and listen. Proverbs 13:20 says, "He who walks with wise men will be wise."[2] You'll be influenced by close proximity to people who've excelled in your area of interest.

For the Christian, it is also vital to listen to God by spending time in prayer and in His word.

Pay attention, and God will give you a dream. God will give you a mental picture of what the future could be. This mental picture is powered by the conviction that the future should be that way. That's vision, and with vision comes purpose.

Proverbs 29:18 says, "Where there is no vision, the people are unrestrained."[3] Without vision there's nothing to work toward. Discipline feels futile. But with vision, you have a purpose and, therefore, a reason to be disciplined.

I enjoy running solo, because it's my time to dream. It's time for God and me. I don't like to wear headphones or have any distractions. I like to just listen. When I run, I experience moments of clarity, which feed my vision for the ministry and my life. Psalm 46:10 says, "Be still, and know I am God."[4] For me running is part of that stillness. Though my body is moving, my mind is still and focused.

Listen to God, and watch for people from whom you can learn. Glean inspiration from both places. Let God cast a vision for you, and then find someone whose accomplishments you admire. Their example will clarify your own vision and solidify your purpose. Walk with people who are wise and learn.

During my years of training and preparation in college and on the book field, I had learned the importance of camaraderie. I knew how much the people around me could influence my growth for better or worse.

Now I was striking out on my own. My prep had been solid, but I felt I had more to learn. I wanted to learn from the best. There were pastors who had accomplished things I admired, the "ultramarathoners" of the independent, church-growth movement. I wanted to know how they'd done it. I wanted to know what it took to grow a church. The best way to find out was to find a way to meet these guys and see their work for myself.

When I finished graduate school, Gayle and I moved to Chicago. One of the ten churches I had read about in *The Ten Largest Sunday Schools* was in the Chicago area. The plan was to work from Chicago and visit all ten of these churches and learn what we could.

We rented a small U-Haul trailer and loaded everything we'd accumulated. By this time, we had a huge Irish Setter. Husker had been a gift from my sister Mary. Since Nebraska had just won the national championship in football in 1970 and 1971, I named our red Irish Setter Husker. We headed for Chicago—Gayle and me in the front seat and the dog in the backseat.

We spent five days in Chicago looking for a place to live. We had been paying $55 a month for rent in Bethany, Oklahoma. When we got to Chicago, we were stunned. Rent was four times that. We were looking at $175-$200 a month, and when potential landlords saw our dog—he was so big his head stuck out one side of the car and his tail out the other side—nobody would even rent to us.

We eventually found a place on the edge of Gary, Indiana. Rent was $165 a month with a $165 deposit. We didn't have that much money, so we had to borrow $300 from Gayle's parents just to get a place to live.

The little house was unfurnished but had a fenced yard where we could put Husker. It had tile floors everywhere: in the bedroom, the living room, dining room, and kitchen. We moved in with almost nothing. We had a card table for a dining table and two trunks for chairs. That was about it. We didn't even have a bed. Since we didn't have money to buy one, we laid all the blankets we owned on the tile floor in the bedroom and slept on those.

I got a job at Youngstown Steel Mill in East Chicago on the graveyard shift. Gayle got a job in a drugstore. I would go to work at night, and when I got home, Gayle would jump in the car and go to work. As soon as we got paid, we found a bed at a garage sale, so we didn't sleep on the floor for too long.

I was absolutely amazed at how much the steel mill paid. I made six dollars an hour. The economy was booming and the mill was busy, so they would often ask us to work overtime. We could get time and a half for overtime, nine dollars an hour. I wanted those hours, but I had to get home so Gayle could take the car and go to her job, which didn't really make sense because my job paid more. We needed to get another set of wheels.

I found an old pickup for sale, a 1956 Ford for $150. I bought it, and I drove that old pickup to work. I worked in the garage in the steel mill, and our job was to keep equipment running. I had the rich experience of working on engines, but I wasn't a mechanic; I was a gopher. I'd "go for" this part or that part. I learned a lot from the mechanics in that garage. When I got the truck, I drove it proudly to work. I thought I got a pretty good deal for $150, but those mechanics looked at my truck and said, "You got took."

I said, "No, no, it's a good truck."

They just smiled. "You got took."

One morning shortly after that, I was driving down the expressway to get home from work, and all of a sudden, I heard steel knocking on steel. I looked in the rearview mirror and smoke was billowing out the back. The engine was shot. About that time, a whole carload of those mechanics went by me and waved. To them it was no big deal, just an old truck, but to Gayle and me it was a huge deal. We were just trying to make it. We had scraped together $150 to buy this truck, so I could work overtime and send $300 dollars back to her mother and daddy and start on our plan to visit churches.

You could hear the truck knocking from two blocks away, but I drove it home—really didn't have any other option. I shut it off, went in the house, and got on my knees by the bed. I cried out to God, "God, here we are trying to make it, trying to learn about building a church for You, and we're doing our best. We bought this truck and now the motor's out. God, you've got to help us." It was all I could think to do.

After pouring out my heart to God, I called Gayle's dad, Gayland. He was a wonderful mechanic and the head service manager of the Buick garage in Guymon. He said, "Sounds like a rod's broken. You'll have to take the pan off and look at the those rods and see which one's broken." So I borrowed a set of tools from somebody, sockets and all. I got under that truck, drained the oil, took the oil pan off, and looked at the rods. To my surprise not one of them was broken.

I called her dad again and told him. He said, "Well, you gotta unhook them from the crank case and check the bearings." Sure enough the insert bearings were shot. I took them out and went to the parts store. I told the guy I needed new insert bearings for a '56 Ford V-8 and showed him what I had. He got me a set and said if I had any trouble to call.

That guy got several calls. Many a time I crawled out from under the truck, went in, and phoned him. I used a rag to keep the grease from getting all over the phone and got his advice as I put the truck together.

Day after day, I'd come home from the steel mill and get under the pickup. I'd lie there for ten minutes thinking before each move I made, because I had never done that kind of repair before. My dog, Husker, would crawl under there with me. I'd think out loud and talk to that dog, "Well, Husker, I think we ought to do this. I think we ought to do that."

I came home one day and told Gayle, "I'm gonna finish the truck today." She went off to work in the car, and I got under that truck and worked all day. In fact, when she came home, I was still under it. When it started getting dark, I was still under the truck. Gayle got an extension cord and trouble light. Before I was done, she was under there helping me hold the oil pan up as I put the bolts back into place. We put the oil in, and with a prayer, we started it. To our surprise, that old truck ran like a sewing machine. I drove it proudly back to the steel mill that night.

The guys at the steel mill were pretty nice to me, though they thought it kind of a strange phenomenon that a guy who was preparing for the ministry would be working there. In fact, they called me "the Parson." That was my nickname.

One of my jobs was to clean the Ross carriers. The Ross carriers carried steel around the plant. They were huge machines, and they would get filthy dirty. The guys would bring them into a great big room to pressure wash them. Being the low man in the garage, I got that job.

One night I was spraying a carrier down. I was wet and covered in muck, and one of the mechanics came in. I could see half a dozen other guys standing over by the coffee pot, and I knew he had been sent as a delegate to ask me a question.

He came up and said, "I have a question to ask you, Parson." He paused, "Did you really graduate from college? Do you really have a college degree?"

I didn't bother to tell him I had a graduate degree as well; I just said, "Yes, I graduated from college."

He said, "Well, then, what the h____ are you doing here?" And he turned and walked away.

I went back to cleaning, but his words stuck in my mind. The devil jumped on my back and said, "What are you doing? You went to school all those years to end up here in a steel mill?" We had come here to learn about church growth, but life had become a matter of survival for us. We were just trying to make it.

It was really a discouraging time. Discouragement like that can be blinding. You can't see anything but what's happening right at that moment—the cramp in your calf or the dirty Ross carrier in front of you and the mechanics behind you laughing. It's vital in those moments to remember your purpose. There in Gary, Indiana, a little voice reminded me that I had a purpose. Our purpose was to learn church growth principles, and we were not to lose sight of that.

One day I got a call from a Nazarene church that was only a mile or two from where we lived in South Gary. The pastor had heard about the work we had done with the children's and bus ministries in a church in Oklahoma City. He asked if I would come over and to help establish their bus ministry. It was common at the time for churches to buy school buses to pick up children from surrounding neighborhoods for Sunday school and church. We spent several Sundays at this church. People were very responsive to the idea of a new ministry, and I was amazed at how well our work there went. Several weeks later he called me and wanted to have lunch. Over lunch, he asked if I'd come on staff full-time. A few days later, I got an offer from John W. Banks to come down to Jasper, Alabama, and serve full-time. Here I was at the steel mill getting these other offers. After working months in the steel mill, that dirty, hot place, I began to think about taking one of those offers.

Yet, it wasn't what we envisioned. These churches were part of the denomination we had grown up in. We wanted to study and understand independent churches. It seemed unwise to turn down any offers, and yet, I wasn't convinced in my gut that these options were best. I did a three-day fast and sought the Lord. At the end of three days, it was very clear to me we were to stay right where we were.

That night, I told Gayle, and she agreed that was the Lord's leading. We decided I would stay on at the steel mill until God moved us elsewhere.

Some weeks before that, I had heard from my friend Alden Laird, the guy who had recruited me to sell at Southwestern. He had gone to Lynchburg, Virginia, because Jerry Falwell was becoming nationally known with his Old-Time Gospel Hour television program and had started Lynchburg Baptist College. Alden was involved with the ministry there and sent me an application to teach at the new college. I filled it out to appease my friend. I didn't think they would be interested in me at all and had almost forgotten about it. Two days after we decided I was going to stay at the steel mill, I got a call from Lynchburg Baptist College. They said they had received my application and asked me to come for an interview.

When I got there, I could not have been more excited to meet Dr. Elmer Towns, the author of the best-selling book *The Ten*

Largest Sunday Schools in America and What Makes Them Grow and cofounder of Lynchburg Baptist College. I interviewed, and they offered me a position teaching English. My mind went back to Greek class and the hours I had spent learning the basics of English so that I could

Carl with Dr. Elmer Towns

learn Greek, and I breathed a prayer of thanks. I went back and resigned at the steel mill.

We built sideboards on the pickup, loaded our furniture in the back, and covered it with a canvas tarp. Gayle drove the car. I drove the pickup. Husker rode with me in the front seat, and we drove all the way to Lynchburg, Virginia.

Lynchburg was Jerry Falwell's hometown. He started Thomas Road Baptist Church in the Donald Duck Bottling Company. From that church came Lynchburg Baptist College, which eventually became Liberty University. Jerry was a man of great faith. He often quoted Jeremiah 32:27, "Behold, I am the Lord, the God of all flesh. Is anything too hard for me?"[5] Jerry's faith was not in what we had but in what God could provide.

There was a spirit of revival and possibility on that campus. Every Monday in my classes, we would have a hard time getting into our lesson, because the kids wanted to share where they had ministered over the weekend and what God was doing.

I taught four English classes and audited two classes under Dr.

Carl with Jerry Falwell

Towns, whose books had so inspired me. In chapel services, Dr. Towns had church planters come and speak. These guys were planting and building a new kind of church. These were independent churches built for growth and agility since they weren't encumbered by heavy denominational ties or traditions. I heard Rudy Holland from Roanoke, Virginia; Bill Monroe from Florence, South Carolina; Bud Calvert from Fairfax, Virginia; and other speakers who inspired and challenged me.

They told how God had called them to start their churches. They explained that their churches were designed for reaching out to the unreached and unchurched. These were Bible-centered, aggressive, cutting-edge churches. When I visited these congregations, I could feel the excitement in the air. People had a sense of purpose. They shared Jesus's passion for the fields white unto harvest.

Dr. Towns was writing a series of articles for *The Sword of the Lord* magazine on great soul-winning churches of America, so he spent his weekends traveling around visiting these churches. Often on Mondays, he would tell us where he had spoken over the weekend.

One day after class, I asked Dr. Towns, "When you go by car, would you mind if I went along and drove for you?" He agreed, and I knew this was the opportunity I had been waiting for. His routine was to go and preach, and after the service, interview the pastor, often over lunch. I got to sit in on these conversations. He'd turn to me during an interview and say, "Carl, do you have some questions for the pastor?" I got to ask some of the most influential pastors in America what made their ministries work. I had been trying to find a way to learn principles of church growth, planning to do it on my own, and here God had made a way for me to learn from the very man whose work had inspired this year of study.

Spending time with Dr. Towns and these men cast a new vision in my mind. I began to see possibilities I hadn't imagined before. As these experiences accumulated, it began to be more and more clear to Gayle and me that God wanted us to plant a church. When we began our one-year study of churches, we intended to learn principles of church growth and go back to our denomination and apply those if we could. But the more we learned about these principles, we began to see that they just wouldn't fit our denominational church. As good as our denomination was—it had taught us the Bible and to know Jesus Christ, and we received our call into the ministry in that church—we also saw that it just was not structured for growth. It would be like taking my pickup and putting it in the Indy 500. It's not gonna win the Indy 500. It's not designed for it; it was designed to haul stuff. The more we thought and prayed about it, we realized that the church we wanted to build had to be independent, designed for growth and outreach.

The next question was, where. I would pace the floor of my office at Lynchburg Baptist College, looking at the map of the United States on the wall and praying, "God, where do you want us to start?" More and more I felt drawn to my hometown, Lincoln, Nebraska, in spite of the fact that God had put a love in my heart for southern people during the summers I spent in Alabama, Georgia, and South Carolina. I knew that the "Bible Belt" had a lot of good, Bible-preaching churches. I wanted to go where the need was great.

I knew my hometown had many mainline denominational churches, but not much in the way of these independent, aggressive, purpose driven ministries that I was studying. I also knew Mom and Dad had been influenced by soul-winning churches and were praying for that type of church in Lincoln.

Jerry Falwell always said, "The difference between mediocrity and greatness in the work of God is vision." He wanted us to be people of vision and knew that heroes of the faith could inspire vision, so he raised money for a spring break trip to England to study the Wesleyan revival.

Dr. Towns believed that John Wesley had influenced his society more for Christ than any other man since the apostle Paul. Wesley literally turned England around. I had been reading about him since college. In fact, when I was in college, I found a set of his works in a used bookstore for $50. That was a whole lot of money then, but I scraped it up and bought that set of Wesley's works and read his journals and sermons.

I couldn't believe I was actually in England where he had lived and ministered, listening to Dr. Towns lecture about his influence. When our tour bus pulled into Bristol, I could see a statue of John Wesley on his horse across the street in front of Wesley Chapel, and I wondered if it was accurate. We got off the bus, crossed the street, and went over to the statue. Sure enough, there in his hand was a little book. I had read how Wesley would give his horse free rein because it was so well trained, and he would read his Bible as he rode.

Just as Wesley's life cast a vision for so many, myself included, heroes in any walk of life can inspire us. The year I spent in Lynchburg learning from those who were experts in my field led to a vision that utterly shaped the ministry we started. God honored our desire to learn from churches we admired and created an opportunity far beyond what I was able to create for myself. The bits of knowledge we gleaned would impact our vision and purpose for the next forty years.

Philippians 1:61[1]

HE WHO BEGAN A GOOD WORK:
THE FIRST YEARS OF MINISTRY | 1973–1975

The congregation viewing the original five acres for the first time

5

PHOENIX, ARIZONA, January 16, 2011. I was right in the middle of the street when it happened. The pain was excruciating. At mile twenty-one of the Phoenix Marathon, I got a severe cramp that felt like a bear had bit me in the leg. I stopped and tried to bend over to rub the calf. When I did, I lost my balance and fell on my backside. Since I couldn't stand, I rolled onto my back and tried to lift my leg up. I must have looked like a flipped beetle.

Before I knew it, emergency guys in red shirts surrounded me. They looked at me with panic as if I had just suffered a heart attack. I told them I was fine but had a terrible cramp. They weren't going to take my word for it, so they helped me off the street. A spectator gave up his chair, and they plopped me down to check my vitals.

When they were sure I wasn't dying, they went to work on my calf.

As they did, one of them said, "Looks like you're done for the day." That put fire in my eyes. All it took was someone telling me I was done and couldn't finish that race to make me get up and shake the pain. I wasn't about to quit.

When I insisted I would finish, he said, "But you can't walk." So I got up and tried to prove I could. I nearly fell again since I couldn't put weight on that leg. I staggered a few steps up the sidewalk, turned around, and came back. They made me sit back down and worked on my leg some more.

I finally convinced them I could walk. When they let me go, I slipped into the crowd of runners and walked as fast as I could until they couldn't see me anymore. I didn't want them to stop me.

As I moved away from the race emergency crew into the crowd of runners, I increased my speed slightly. Soon I saw mile marker twenty-two, and it hit me. I had 4.2 miles to keep going through this pain, and all I could manage was a slow dog-trot. My time was shot, and I still had four miles to struggle through. Miserable feeling.

The best reason to keep going at a time like that is to know you've worked too hard to quit. I reminded myself of the mornings I got up when it was dark and was running before the sun came up. I run outside with my dog, Scout, as often as I can, and I thought of those runs in the bitter, cold Nebraska weather, facing that biting north wind and hearing the snow crunch under my feet. When I crest the hill on Bluff Road and look east, I can often see the orange ball of the sun peeking over the horizon. To the north, a farmhouse is tucked away in the trees. I love that scene. I've seen it in the early morning in every season of the year. In winter, everything's white with snow. In the summer, the green fields of corn are already "knee-high by the Fourth of July." My mind went back to those training runs down the road from my house. I had put too much in to quit.

Even if my time was shot, people were going by me, and I felt humiliation, I was going to finish. I didn't want a Did Not Finish (DNF) by my name. I kept picking them up and putting them down and finished those four miles. You'd better believe I felt like quitting, but I told myself runners don't quit. We hit the wall. We fade, but we keep on going.

At the finish of the Phoenix Marathon, they put that medal over my head, and even though my time was four hours and thirty-some minutes, I knew what I had gone through to get that medal. In my heart, I felt accomplishment and victory.

Life, too, is full of pain and challenges. People come into our church week after week, and I see it on their faces—the desire to quit mixed with the determination to keep going. I pray every week that those who come with heavy hearts and struggles will leave with new hope. I want them to feel wanted, loved, and accepted in our church family. I hope the promises of God will give them power to go out and face difficult situations and keep on going—just keep on keeping on.

The challenges we encounter in life are no reason to quit the journey. It's easy to feel that challenges mean failure. In fact, they mean just the opposite. They are the opportunity to persevere and find strength you never knew you had. Just as resistance generates muscle, working through our worst experiences generates strength of character and joy in our lives. God will provide the strength. Philippians 4:13 says, "I can do all things through Christ who strengthens me."[2]

I hope Calvary reflects that truth. Our journey hasn't been perfect, but I hope we are stronger because of that. In forty years of ministry, we have faced many challenges. Especially in the early years, there were days I felt I'd be doing everyone a favor if I quit. I felt that despite all the work I'd done to get there, I was failing. I couldn't keep the pace I had started with. But I stayed, however unwillingly. We're all works in progress, though, and "He who began a good work... will continue it."[3] Forty years in, I can say that God has indeed continued His work from the humble beginning.

Home of Roy & Alice Godwin where we met three weeks to plan and pray

When the school year was over at Lynchburg Baptist College, Gayle and I once again packed our car and headed west, home to Lincoln, Nebraska. My parents were supportive of our vision to plant a church. For the first three Sundays, Mom and Dad, Eva, a friend of the family, and Gayle and I met in my parents' living room to pray and plan. Our first meeting was June 10, 1973, which happened to be my twenty-sixth birthday.

In preparation for our first organized Sunday service, we rented a meeting room in the Christian Record Braille Building, which was owned by the Seventh Day Adventists. We knocked on doors the entire week before our first Sunday to get the word out about our new church. Gayle's parents and Howard Day, my roommate and friend from college, even came to help. It felt like we knocked on every door in the surrounding area that week, and we were ready for a good crowd on Sunday.

Christian Record Braille entrance where people entered through garage

Sunday came, and we started with Sunday school. I was utterly dismayed. Besides our family and friends, there were four or five other people. After all that work, almost no one had come. Then after Sunday school, we went to open the doors for the church service, and there they were—a line of people waiting to come in. Fifty-two people came to church that morning. It was so uplifting for me. Howard led music, and I preached and felt like a real pastor. Many came out of curiosity to see our first Sunday, but the next week twenty-seven of them came back and several kept coming.

For the first year, the church could not financially support me. Gayle worked as an accountant at the Lincoln Public School administrative building. My job was to get the word out. The only way I knew to do that was to walk the neighborhoods and knock on doors. My time selling books for Southwestern became more relevant than I could have dreamed, as day after day I took material about our church and knocked on door after door. Every time I started a new block, I would stand at the corner, look at the row of houses, and pray, "Lord, help me find at least one person interested in finding a church."

I could determine right away if people were interested. If they weren't, I would hand them some material with the gospel and move on to the next door, searching for people who were receptive to hearing about a new church plant. When I found them, I told them about our vision and asked if I could send them our newsletter. I was building a mailing list. Of course, this was long before email and even before personal computers, but we had a mimeograph machine. Once a month we mimeographed the newsletter and mailed it out to update people on the church's progress.

I knocked on doors that whole summer and preached on Sundays, and then September 19, 1973, Dr. Elmer Towns came for our organizational service. He read the items of the charter for the congregation. When he got to the item of pastor, he asked if they agreed that Carl Godwin should be pastor and shepherd of this flock. There was a unanimous "Amen." A lifelong dream was coming true, and I was overcome and grateful.

That night eighteen people signed the charter as members. I stood up and told them that one day God would give us about twenty acres. We would have buildings. We would have ministries for children. We would have ministries for teenagers, young adults, and adults. We would have a church staff. Most people looked at me like a cow looks at the new gate, skeptical at best. After all, we were meeting in a rented building; we didn't have any specialized ministries and couldn't support the one pastor we had. It's no wonder people had a little trouble with that vision, and I would too before it was all over.

The first year of the church was so exciting. Week by week we had new faces. On our first anniversary, we had over 100 people. Soon, we outgrew the rooms we had been renting at the Christian Record Braille Building, so we moved to the Southeast YMCA.

The Y was an old building that had been a dairy farm years before. It still occupied seven acres, but the city had grown around it. It had

VBS at the Southeast YMCA

eighteen-inch thick walls, so even though it didn't have air conditioning, it stayed cool. The building provided a large meeting room for church and numerous other rooms we used for gatherings and classes.

The owners of the building gave us permission to put up a sign that said, "Temporary Site of Bible Baptist Church, Pastor Carl Godwin." That sign gave me chills. It was so exciting for me to read "Pastor Carl Godwin." I would go out of my way to drive past the building just so I could see that sign.

There was one problem with our new location. One Sunday morning I was setting up chairs for the service, and Gayle was back in the kitchen making Kool-Aid for Sunday school. I heard a blood-curdling scream. Man, I dropped the chair I was holding and ran back to the kitchen thinking somebody had attacked my wife. When I got there, she was up on a chair and gasped, "A mouse."

After that on Sunday mornings, somebody'd be helping me set up chairs for church, and we'd hear a scream come from the kitchen. I would just say, "Don't worry about it. It happens every week." Often I would be preaching away, and all of a sudden, I'd hear people on the front row squeal and lift their feet as a mouse shot by.

During the second year of our church, a retired minister started attending. We had about sixteen families by then, and he befriended our families and was very influential. He bought us hymnals, and I asked him to teach now and then. After awhile, he began to find fault with my leadership. I was doing the best I could, having never led a church before. He influenced some families, and five families left our church.

Losing those families took the wind out of our sails. The momentum we had seemed to go. When you are a church plant with no buildings, no staff, no property, and people are driving by churches with all those things

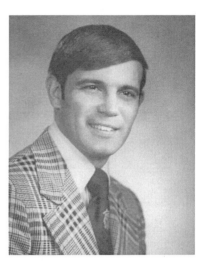

Picture of Carl that was on our first flyer that we distributed

to come to your church, they're really only coming for one reason. They are coming because of vision and excitement for the future. When you lose that, you have lost the most essential thing a church plant can have. Losing five families doesn't sound like a lot, but when you only have fifteen or sixteen families, it makes a big difference. People could feel it.

On our second anniversary, we tried to have a big day like our first, but our numbers had dwindled to about half of what we'd had. It seemed to go from bad to worse. The weeks went by and turned into months, and we just couldn't get it turned around. You could feel the discouragement in the air. We had definitely lost our momentum.

I spent whole nights over at the Y building praying. It was quiet and hollow there at night. I would kneel on those red exercise mats and beg God to turn things around, but nothing changed. Finally, I was convinced we had made a mistake. God must not have wanted us in Lincoln. I decided that night to quit. I thought God must have some other ministry for us some place else. Persistence seemed like foolishness.

With that decision made, I went to bed and slept. I got up the next morning, went to shave, and there, taped to the mirror, was a piece of paper with Bible verses on it. It had been there for several weeks, actually, but it was as if I'd never read it before. It was I Corinthians 15:57–58, "But thanks be unto God, who gives us the victory through our Lord Jesus Christ. Therefore, my beloved brethren, be steadfast, immovable, always abounding in the work of the Lord, knowing that your toil is not in vain in the Lord."[4] I was convinced our labor was in vain, and there was no point. Pain and fatigue had buried the vision I had attached to until it had all but disappeared. But God said to be unmovable, always abounding in the work of the Lord.

My tears mixed with the shaving cream as I said, "Okay, God, I'll stay. If I have to set up folding chairs in a rented building for the rest of my life, I'll stay." I wasn't very happy about it, but I said, "Yes, God, I'll stay."

Don't get me wrong, I didn't have a moment of vision in which I saw things change and my hopes become reality, but I did have a moment of faith—a reminder that the reasons I had started this ministry were still there and still good. The substance of the work was the same and that was reason to hope. I had worked too hard in my prep, and God had given me this vision. There was no quitting even though the pain was severe.

During this time, we had the church treasurer and his wife over to our house after church one Sunday night. While we were visiting, Gayle said, "You know, I'm praying that God will give our church $25,000." I about fell out of my chair. That was more than the church's annual income. Where would we ever get $25,000? Surely even God couldn't afford $25,000. But she made it clear, she was praying for $25,000 for our church.

We had been looking for land so we could build a church building and have a permanent location. We'd found property on the south side of Lincoln. My dad, Gayle, and I went out to see it. It was a beautiful piece of land. We prayed and hoped we could get it.

I called the developer and said, "Bill, we'd be interested in buying that land."

"Well, I sold it to the Catholics," he replied.

We found another property. This was a beautiful piece, and I was just sure this was the one. On a Wednesday night, the men of the church loaded in the van and drove out there. I think there were eight of us. We stood and looked out over the city. We prayed over that land and claimed it for God.

Again, I called Bill and said, "Bill, we really are interested in that piece."

He replied, "You know what, I sold it to the Seventh Day Adventists."

I began to feel like there was no land left for us. I went home and knelt by my bed and cried out, "God, what about us? We're still meeting in a rented building. Please hear our prayer and provide a place for our ministry."

Sometime later I got a call from Bill. He said, "I know you were disappointed about those properties, but I do have a piece of land out on First and Superior Streets, in the northwest part of the city." He said, "I would be willing to sell you five acres out there for $5,000 an acre."

I thought, *The northwest part of the city? We're located in the southeast corner of the city. That is clear across town.* But I said I'd look. Gayle and I drove out in our little Volkswagen bug. We took Interstate 180, got off on Cornhusker Highway, went west to First Street, and turned north on First. At Benton Road, the pavement ended and we hit gravel. I said to Gayle, "This is plumb out in the country." After a mile on the gravel, we came to the property. We turned in and drove up on the hill. The grass was knee high. I remember Gayle was pregnant with our first baby. I can picture her getting out of the car and walking with me in the tall grass.

I said, "You know, this is a pretty hill." I looked over to the east and could see Interstate 180 going north and south, in and out of the city. I could look northwest and see Interstate 80 going east and west across the north part of the city.

We walked over to an old mulberry tree by the fence row where a farmer had left a bale of straw, knelt down by that bale at the foot of the tree, and prayed, "God, if you'd give us this property, and if you'd let us, we will spend our lives here building a church for You."

I called Bill and told him we were interested in the property. He said, "Well, I'm trying to get it rezoned. If the City Council will rezone it, Farm Bureau Insurance Company wants to buy it. If I can't get it rezoned for them to buy it, I'd be happy to sell you part of it. There are sixteen acres there in that corner. I will sell you five acres if Farm Bureau can't get it rezoned."

I found out when the City Council was meeting, and I was there. At one o'clock Farm Bureau's attorney presented the case and asked that the sixteen acres that make up the corner at First and Superior Streets be rezoned. I thought the City Council would vote right away. I didn't know they heard all the issues first and voted on them later in the day. So, I sat on the back row of the City Council chamber and waited. I heard all the different issues presented that day, and I waited.

As time went by, I got a little anxious. I opened my Bible and thought, *Well, God, give me something.* I opened to Psalm 37 without realizing that in that Psalm the psalmist is writing about the Promised Land. Six times he mentions "the land." In verse three it says, "Trust the Lord and do good. Dwell in the land and cultivate faithfulness." In verse nine: "But, those who wait for the Lord, they will inherit the land." Verse eleven: "But the humble will inherit the land." Verse twenty-two: "For those blessed by Him will inherit the land." Verse twenty-nine: "The righteous will inherit the land." Verse thirty-four: "Wait for the Lord and keep His way and He will exalt you to inherit the land."[5] I closed my Bible with a new calm assurance.

Finally, it was time for the council to vote. As they began, my heart was racing. The vote went: one to rezone, one no, another yes, another no, another yes for rezoning, another no. Three for rezoning, three opposed. Then came the seventh and final vote, no. It was not rezoned.

I called Bill and asked if we could have a meeting. We sat down over coffee, and I shared our dream and vision of building a church and reaching people for Jesus Christ. I asked, "Bill, would you be willing to donate half that property, half of those five acres, to us?"

There was a moment of hesitation, which seemed like an eternity to me. Then Bill said, "Yes, I could do that."

Now, instead of needing $25,000, we needed $12,500. I met with our people and told them we had an opportunity to buy five beautiful acres for $12,500. We had saved $2,000 and that had taken us three years. Now, we needed to raise $10,500 quickly. One Sunday night, we loaded the whole congregation into two school buses and drove across town. We drove up on the hill and showed them the land. Our people loved it and were excited. We raised the $10,500 and paid

*Excited son and mother,
Carl and Alice, on our hill*

Bill $12,500. It dawned on me that God had answered Gayle's prayer and had just given our church $25,000.

Often as we start on a journey toward a goal, we run into obstacles. Those obstacles can be painful, but God asks us to keep going. We have to take that first step and then the next, and only then can we see the finish ahead. But there's the time between the stepping and the seeing. That's where fear comes in and pain can derail us. It's tempting to quit but don't. Lean into each step. There's a finish line ahead. He who began the work will continue it and give you strength.

A HERO'S HUG:
FAMILY SHAPES MINISTRY | 1976–1980

1980 | Carl and Gayle with Carla, Nathan, and Carey

6

CHICAGO, ILLINOIS, October 12, 2003. Though I had promised myself my first marathon would also be my last, after a few weeks the soreness worked out of my legs, and I was ready to put on my running gear and get out and run some more. I had a sweet taste in my mouth from that first marathon. I had felt the thrill of pushing my body to an extreme it had never felt and crossing the finish line. As Emil Zátopek, 1952 Olympic Marathon Gold Medalist, said, "If you want to win something, run 100 meters. If you want to experience something, run a marathon."[1] As the weeks went by, I forgot the pain and remembered the experience.

So despite my promise that I would never do it again, I signed up for the Chicago Marathon. My sister Martha and brother-in-law

Larry live in Chicago. Larry is a pastor, too, and we always have great fellowship, so we stayed with them. This time I checked the elevation map, and the course was as flat as a tabletop. I didn't want to battle hills.

I sat down with my planner and penciled in my plan for the next four months of training. That penciled in plan became my boss. Every week, I reviewed it and reevaluated the training runs I had scheduled. After I actually ran the miles, I would go over my pencil number with a pen. Recording my progress motivated me as I counted down to the race on the calendar.

Eleven months after the Kansas City marathon, I found myself in line with a mass of humanity as 40,000 runners waited to start the Chicago Marathon. When the gun went off, I was so many blocks behind the starting line that it took me six minutes just to get to it. Of course, I had a microchip on my shoe, as all the runners did, so race officials could record the exact time it took me to go from the starting line to the finish line.

As I ran, I was amazed at the spectators. They lined the course, mile after mile, four and five feet deep on each side of the street. The bridges were the only places without spectators, and we crossed several as we wound through downtown Chicago.

We went north past Moody Church and Bible Institute, and I thought of D.L. Moody, the great gospel preacher of over 100 years ago. His revivals and preaching in Chicago and around the world reached many people for Jesus Christ. As I ran I prayed that God would use me like he used D.L. Moody. We looped around and came back on the west side of Moody Church and went right into downtown, where skyscapers cast shadows on the course.

At mile ten, I still hadn't seen Gayle or the rest of my curb crew. Our daughter Carey and her son Wesley were there along with

Martha and Larry. I didn't see any of them. I kept looking mile after mile, wondering where they were.

At the halfway mark I was keeping a good pace, but still hadn't seen my family. By miles eighteen and nineteen, I felt good, but I was really looking for my family. I was looking on both sides of the street and couldn't see them anywhere.

As I came into Chinatown at mile twenty, I saw somebody ahead slip under the yellow, plastic tape that marks the course and keeps the spectators back. Sure enough, it was Carey. After twenty miles of running, she was a welcome sight.

Gayle was back in the crowd with little Wesley, but Carey had seen me coming and wasn't going to let me miss them. The roar of the crowd and the band playing in Chinatown were so loud I couldn't hear a thing, but I could see her with her arms waving. She was cheering and yelling for me. I stopped pumping my arms for a moment, spread them wide, and ran into her hug.

"You're looking good, Dad," she said.

"I'm feeling good," I said. "I love you. I'll see you at the finish."

She said, "Love you, Dad."

Off I went, wiping tears from my eyes. It meant so much after twenty miles of running to see my daughter and get a hug from her. I don't think I could explain to her or anybody how much it meant. When you are trying to accomplish something daunting and you get encouragement and love from your family, it's unspeakable. That hug from Carey told me she believed in me.

A lot of us grow up with a desire to be a hero and to do something significant. I remember as a little boy listening to the Lone Ranger on the radio. Who was that masked man? I wanted to grow up and be that hero and help people like the Lone Ranger. But you grow up, and you're not famous, and you don't seem to be able to make a big difference. You're just an everyday person, common as grass. Still there's one place you can be a hero, and that's behind your front door with your family.

On the bookshelf in my office, I keep a card Carey sent me some years ago for Father's Day. The front is a picture of a dad with his little girl. They're dancing, and she's standing on the toes of his shoes, looking up at him. It says, "How do you know if a man is a hero?" Inside it says, "Ask him if he has a daughter." To think that I could be her hero. There are a lot of things in life that I can't and won't be, but for one instant in Chicago, I felt like a hero.

I told Carey I was feeling good, but a couple miles later, the pain set in. I remember thinking, *I've got four more miles to finish, and I cannot let up. I've got to keep up this pace.* Running a marathon is really very simple. You just run until you can't run anymore, and then you run some more.

Finally, I crossed mile marker twenty-six and had the great feeling of knowing I had only 385 yards to go. The finish at Chicago was magnificent. There was a huge crowd in the stands. They cheered for us all also-rans as if we were the world-famous elites. I finished in 4:15. When they put that medal over my head, it was that sweet finish-line-feeling and the flood of emotion again. This time it was really special because I had had a hero's hug at mile twenty to help me finish.

When I set out to start a church, I was young and ambitious. Gayle and I didn't have children. I believed with all my heart in the work we were doing. As time went on and we began to have a family, the temperature of that work changed. I was committed not just to my congregation but also to my family. That commitment brought joys and responsibilities I had not anticipated, but I believe having a family enriched my view of ministry. It helped me see how our people needed support during the week.

We started Parkview Christian School to meet those needs. We envisioned and finally built a Family Life Center to support daily community within our church. These new visions brought their own challenges. At times it felt that those challenges were more than I could bear, but I had three little ones who needed me to be strong.

If you have kids, you know that parenting is perhaps the one thing for which you can't quite prepare. From the time we had Carey, I was struck by how different raising children was from any other work I'd done. I knew how to work hard and persevere where ministry was concerned, but kids are different. I'm still not sure I've figured parenting out, but it certainly changed my life and the course of ministry.

Early one Saturday morning in May of 1976, Gayle shook me awake urgently, "Carl, it's time to go."

From a dead sleep, I mumbled, "Go where? I want to go back to sleep."

"No, wake up. The baby's coming."

It finally registered, and I jumped out of bed and went running around the house trying to get ready. Of course, she was calm. Her bags were packed and ready to go. We jumped in the car, and I sped toward the hospital.

I don't do well in hospitals—a phobia that made me question my pastoral ambitions in the very beginning—and this was going to be no exception. During the pregnancy we tried to go to Lamaze class. At the first class, the teacher said, "We're going to show you a film about delivery, and after the film, we will have some refreshments and take questions." Well, goodness, the film was of an actual delivery. I don't know what I expected, but it wasn't that. My stomach started turning, and I was sweating. I slid down in my seat and put my hand up on my forehead to stop the spinning. Gayle noticed my condition and made me put my head between my knees. Tell you what, I didn't want refreshments after that. We snuck out before the movie even ended.

It was a new thing in those days for daddies to go in the delivery room. When she was ready to take Gayle back, the nurse asked, "Is he coming with us?"

My wife just laughed and said, "He couldn't make it through Lamaze class. There's no way he's coming in with us."

The nurse's name was Margie. I'll never forget her. She was a solid woman with an air of authority. Margie looked at me with amused condescension and threw a gown at me. She directed, "Put this on just in case you change your mind."

I said, "Yes, ma'am," and put it on. Then I sat down and waited. I waited and waited, and my thoughts went back to all the changes in our lives: finishing our education, getting married, selling books for Southwestern, the steel mill, getting to know Dr. Towns and studying churches, leaving our denomination, planting an autonomous church, acquiring land for that church, and now perhaps the biggest change, becoming a daddy.

In my ministry, I was in the middle of what I had imagined— actually running the race I had prepared for for so long. It's strange to look up mid-race like that and realize it's happening. The thing for which you've trained is underway. There's a kind of elation. But parenting, there was no way to prepare for that.

About that time Margie came out and ordered, "All right, come with me."

I was uneasy, but I said, "Yes, ma'am," and followed her into the delivery room.

She slapped a stool and said, "Siddown on that right there," so I sat down beside Gayle and held her hand. They told her to push, and just like that, the baby was here. They had waited until the last moment to fetch me. Gayle had done the hard work already; I got there for the payoff. They brought that beautiful baby, our first baby girl, Carey, and put her in my arms. I felt the presence of God. It was like watching creation. I felt like I could just reach out with my hand and touch God.

I went home that morning and called every family in the church. Now, that wasn't that many calls. I think we only had about twenty families, but I phoned every one. It was Saturday morning; I was going to see them the next day, but I couldn't wait to tell them we had a baby girl. Of course, the next day they were all in church because they wanted to see what proud papa Pastor Carl looked like.

After Carey was born, the ladies of the church had a baby shower, and they all went together and got Gayle and me a beautiful rocking chair. It was wooden and had cushions tied to it. We brought it home and put in our living room. It looked a little out of place next to our old, ugly couch.

One day Gayle came home and said, "Honey, I found the couch that matches that chair. They're a set." I agreed that our old couch was ugly, so we went to see the couch. The salesperson said it was the last one, and it was discontinued. Then I asked how much. The couch was $300. Oh, my lands! We didn't have $30 let alone $300.

I told the salesperson we needed a minute, and I said to Gayle, "Honey, we can't finance a couch."

"But it's the last one." I could see how badly she wanted it.

I said, "We'll have to pray. God's got to provide the money."

Well, when my wife starts praying, God begins to move. I had no idea where we would get an extra $300. We had no means of extra income at all, but she was praying.

Later that week, I got a phone call from my dad. Dad was working up at Prudhoe Bay, Alaska, on the oil pipeline. He said, "We have a group of believers here, sort of a little church, and we want to know if you would come up and preach a series of services for us." So I flew up and preached four nights to the day crew and three mornings to the night crew.

I'll never forget getting off the plane at Prudhoe Bay. When the doors opened, the wind hit my lungs, and they felt like they froze instantly. The cold took my breath away. It was February, and it was not unusual to have whiteouts where you couldn't see ten feet in front of your face. The snow wasn't just on the roofs of buildings; it was on the sides, because it blew across so hard and fast that it stuck to vertical surfaces.

While I was there, a security guard came to the services. One night he asked me if I'd like to ride with him while he did his shift. We went out in his truck, keeping an eye on things at Prudhoe Bay. Pretty soon we got a call on the radio. One of the security guys said, "Hey, did you look up? Look up." It was a very still night, colder than you could ever imagine, probably thirty-five degrees below zero, but completely still. We stepped out of the truck, snow crunching under our boots. We looked up, and there were the northern lights. It looked like if you had a twenty-foot extension ladder you could climb right up and touch them. They were right above us like curtains of different colors just waving in the air.

When the week finished, they passed the hat. I hoped that they would be able to give me enough to cover my flight, which was well over $600. I was blown away. They not only paid my flight, but they paid me $800 above my expenses.

I flew home, and Gayle picked me up at the airport. When I got in the car, I said, "Honey, do you suppose the furniture store still has

Carey "reading" to baby sister, Carla, while sitting on our "answer to prayer" couch

that couch?" We drove straight to the store, didn't even go home, and there was the couch. I paid the man cash over the barrel for that couch, and we both knew that God had heard and answered our prayers and supplied again for us.

Our third anniversary as a church was the perfect time to make the move from meeting in the Y building in southeast Lincoln to a new location in the northwest part of the city near the land we had purchased. People told us we couldn't move our congregation clear across town. They warned we'd lose our people. I felt strongly, however, that people don't just attend the church that is nearest; they attend the church that is dearest. We also knew that a move of such significance would be what we made it to be, and we decided to make it a grand occasion.

We planned a land dedication service on our five acres. We rented a large tent and chairs and invited Mayor Helen Boosalis and Husker quarterback Tom Sorley to speak. I walked the neighborhoods near the land everyday that week, knocking on doors and telling our story. Some of our congregation came and helped in the evenings. We did our best to let everyone in northwest Lincoln know about our big third anniversary tent service that Sunday.

After knocking doors all day, I would go to the park next to our land and spend the last hour of the evening walking and praying. I prayed that God would bless our efforts and that our church and our people would change this corner of the city. I prayed that people would be reached for God.

On a good Sunday in the Y building, our attendance was about eighty people, but on our third anniversary, we were dumbfounded as 185 people packed the tent. Mayor Helen Boosalis brought a word

Dale Markussen, Terry Boss, Gayland Wooldridge, and Ron Dooley move the piano for the Third Anniversary tent service

of congratulations and welcome. Quarterback Tom Sorley shared his testimony. Then, with great enthusiasm, I shared our dream of building a ministry to reach many for Christ. This was by far our greatest Sunday yet and was no doubt the turning point we needed.

The years continued to be tight financially for Gayle and me, but God never failed to provide for our family. We had our second daughter, Carla, in August of 1978. When we brought her home, Carey ran back and forth between her room and where Carla was on the sofa, stacking every doll she had around that baby. Most of the dolls were bigger than Carla, but Carey was ready to share every last one with her baby sister. This began a lifelong friendship between the two of them.

That same year, we found out my mom had a large brain tumor. We took her to the Mayo Clinic in Rochester, Minnesota, where she would have surgery to remove the tumor. Late the night before surgery, the rest of the family had left the room, but I sat by her bed.

We read the Bible together and talked about being strong in faith.

Around 11:00 p.m., a new shift of nurses came on duty, and a nurse came in Mom's room and said, "Mrs. Godwin, it's late. Visiting hours are passed, and your family will need to leave."

Without hesitation Mom replied, "Oh, this is my pastor."

The nurse apologized and left. Mom and I just grinned at each other.

Being called "Pastor Carl" is music to my ears. I love to hear someone say of me "this is my pastor." To hear my mother say it was a great honor.

Our family and the church joined in prayer for Mom as she underwent major surgery. Though nerve damage left her appearance changed, we were so grateful that she survived and that the tumor was gone.

Around the same time, Gayle's dad had triple by-pass surgery. How strange it was to begin to worry over our parents' health. He recovered, and we were grateful.

Then in 1980, we rejoiced in the birth of our son, Nathan. These changes in our family and the purchase of the land in northwest Lincoln prompted us to sell the house we lived in on South 15th Street and purchase a home in a new subdivision called the Highlands, which was located across the interstate from our church property.

After our third anniversary tent service, we moved the congregation to the Belmont Community Center just a couple miles from our five acres. Meeting there was great motivator for us to get going on a building. The Community Center had an over-head heater right behind the pulpit. It often kicked on during sermons and roared like a freight train. For all its roaring, the heat stayed ceiling high and never got down to the floor, so everybody had cold feet but a hot head. It was not a pleasant place.

We needed $110,000— a lot of money in those days—to start our building. We put together a portfolio that showed the growth of our church over its four-year history, and we went to bank after bank trying to secure a loan. No bank was willing to loan us the money. These rejections

We moved northwest to meet in the Belmont Community Center when land was purchased on our hill.

turned out to be a blessing in disguise. When we couldn't get a loan, we decided to eliminate the middleman of the bank and go straight to people. We decided to sell bonds.

When you borrow from a bank, you're really borrowing from people of the community who have their money in savings in the bank. The bank pays them two percentage points, at least, less than they charge you for the loan, and that's how they make money. At that time it would have cost us nine and a half percent to borrow money from a bank, so we sold our bonds for eight and a half percent interest, which saved us a percent of interest. The eight and a half was a percent higher than most people would have made on their savings. We saved a percentage point, and people made a percent more.

The bank did serve as what was called a paying agent. We made our payment to the bank every week. Our payments were $250 a week, which seemed huge. If we missed one, we were in trouble, but we never missed a payment over the fifteen years of the bonds.

We had $110,000 worth of bonds to sell, and a two-week campaign to do it in. Near the end of those two weeks, we had almost accomplished the task. We only had a few bonds yet to sell, but we had talked to everybody we knew. I knew of no one else to talk to. I got on my knees that Saturday morning and prayed about it. I said, "Lord, I don't know who else to talk to. We still have bonds to sell, and I would sure like to have them all sold by tomorrow and be able to stand and tell our people every bond is sold."

I had a thought that was almost like a voice—I believe it was God's direction, "Just go down your street and knock on doors and talk to people." I was used to knocking on doors to sell books or to share our story and invite people to church, but to knock on doors to see if somebody would buy a bond? It seemed a little strange, but I did it.

I started knocking on doors on our street, and when I got to the third door, Mrs. Snyder acted as if she was expecting me. She told me to come in and asked what we had available. I told her and explained how the bonds worked. She wrote a check for the two largest bonds we had left.

As I was putting the papers away about ready to leave, that same urging voice that sent me knocking on doors prompted me to speak to her about eternity. I said, "Mrs. Snyder, there's something more important than raising money and building the church building and that is your eternal destiny, where you're going to spend your eternity. Do you know for sure that Heaven is your eternal home, Mrs. Snyder? Do you know for sure that if you died today you would go to Heaven?"

She looked at me and said, "No, I don't know that for sure."

I told her that the good news of the Bible is that you can know for sure, "These things I have written to you . . . so that you may know that you have eternal life."[2] That's why the Bible was written. The Bible also tells us that we're all sinners, there's a penalty on our sin, and Jesus Christ, God's son, paid the penalty on the cross for us so that we can have the assurance of eternal life and be born into the family of God. I shared that with Mrs. Snyder and asked her if she would like to invite Jesus to be her personal Savior. She bowed her head with me and prayed a prayer inviting Jesus to come into her life, trusting Him for her salvation.

Mrs. Snyder worked on Sundays and couldn't often come to church. Since we had moved and were no longer neighbors, I was surprised when one day after the service, a lady in our church named Linda came up to me and said, "Did you know that Mrs. Snyder is in the hospital and is dying?"

That week, I went to visit her. When I arrived at the hospital, Linda was there. She told me, "She's in a coma now and won't be able to respond to you, but before she went into coma, I asked her about her salvation. She said, 'Oh, I am ready to go to Heaven. Pastor Carl shared with me how I could know that Heaven is my eternal home, and I invited Jesus Christ to be my Savior.'" Then Linda said, "I am so glad I got the message to you that she was interested in buying bonds and that you went to see her."

I was surprised. I had never received a message about selling bonds to Mrs. Snyder. I said, "I never got that message."

She said, "Why, I left a message at the office for you."

"No, I never got it," I told her. "I got up that morning and prayed, and God led me to go down the street knocking on doors. It makes sense now, though, that when I got to Mrs. Snyder's, she seemed to be expecting me." We were both amazed at how God works.

In 1979 construction began on our first building. I think the

First Building complete

construction crew felt like celebrities because we were there almost every day taking pictures. We couldn't have been more elated to watch a building going up. Every Sunday there was excitement in the air. God was sending us new people.

We began meeting in our building in the fall of 1979. That first Sunday was indescribable. After meeting in rented buildings for four and half years, we had a place of our own. Finally, there was a feeling of permanence. We had a place to hang our hat.

Many of our people worked long and hard the Saturday before our first service in the new building to get it ready. In fact, we were a little afraid that the paint might not be dry in time for church. Our light fixtures hadn't been delivered yet so we had bare light bulbs hanging from the ceiling. I remember looking out from the pulpit and seeing two rows of light bulbs hanging over the pews and still thinking that auditorium was one of the best things I'd ever seen.

Mayor Boosalis came again and congratulated us, saying she never thought we'd accomplish this in the less than two years since our land dedication.

Our property was not on a paved road. The road was gravel, and when we got spring rains, it was almost impassable. You didn't have to have a four-wheel-drive to come to our church, but it helped.

There were times when the road was literally closed due to mud, and people had to drive around a road-closed sign to get to church. We were very thankful a few years later when it was paved even though we were assessed over $50,000.

Road closed

By 1980 we were growing so quickly we couldn't build fast enough to hold the crowd. I got Elmer Towns' tape series on how to go to two services. Without having to build another square-foot of building, we could double our capacity. We implemented the change and had an early church service, then Sunday school, and then the second service. I would preach, teach the adult Bible class, and then preach again. Then I'd do the Sunday evening service and speak on Wednesday nights as well. I look back at the load I carried and wonder how in the world I did it.

We had been building our bus ministry and were bringing in kids from all the surrounding neighborhoods for Sunday school. That year we won the Fastest Growing Sunday School Award for the state of Nebraska from the International Christian Education Association. Gayle and I flew to Detroit, Michigan, to the national conference and received the award. We received it two years running.

The church was also honored to be featured in Dr. Towns' book *Getting a Church Started in the Face of Insurmountable Odds with Limited Resources in Unlikely Circumstances*,[3] which told the stories of several church plants. Our story focused on our decision to move to my hometown and start a ministry with nothing but a calling.

The load was becoming so heavy that we decided to call our first staff member. Assistant Pastor Bob Winebarger came to us from Grand Island, Nebraska. I had visited and preached at his church. When I heard he wanted to move on from his church in Grand Island, I talked to him about serving with us. The Winebargers came and worked with us for thirteen years and could not have been a better addition to help us to build a church. Bob's gifts complemented mine. He was a great Bible teacher, counselor, and organizer. His wife, Karen, was an outstanding asset, and their daughters and ours became good friends.

Since our five acres were a bit removed from the corner where First and Superior Streets meet, I was greatly concerned that if the land around us was developed we would become landlocked. I called Bill, who had sold us the original five acres, and asked him about the surrounding eleven acres that made up the corner of First and Superior Streets. Bill sent me a plot with a street going in and cul-de-sacs and lots for houses. Bill said they would be happy to sell us some lots. Oh, that was a distressing thought to me. We didn't just need to buy some lots around our five acres and expand an acre or two; we needed the whole eleven acres. I presented that to Bill and pressed him for all eleven acres, and after much discussion, he agreed to sell them to us.

Again, our people rose to the occasion and sold bonds. We were able to acquire the eleven acres surrounding our five giving us a sixteen-acre corner. Sometime later, we also acquired the twenty acres to the south from Bill, which gave us a total campus area of thirty-six acres.

111

Our bus and children's ministries kept growing and were becoming more than Bob and I could manage in addition to our other responsibilities. Someone in our church told me about a man in St. Louis who was great with children and worked in a church there. We contacted John Brooks.

As a young man, John had been quite a rounder and a drinker. He had ruined his first marriage. His second wife was at her wit's end and was about ready to leave him when John came to know Jesus Christ as his personal Savior and gave his life to God. His life changed dramatically, his marriage healed, and John began to serve in a church. John did not have formal education or formal training in the Bible, but he had something that education and training couldn't give you. He had an amazing heart for people. I've never seen a man who had such a way of winning people to himself.

We brought John on staff. The boys and girls loved him. He knew how to get to their hearts. More than once in staff meeting, I read a note from a teacher about a child repeatedly acting up in class and told John, "We can't have one person disturbing the whole class so others can't learn and hear the Bible. We've got do something about this young man. His teacher suggests that we don't let him come anymore."

He'd ask for the boy's name and would go by that week and visit with the family. He'd come back and tell me the stories. "Well, the boy's father is an alcoholic, and his mother is struggling to keep it all

Carey, Jennifer Winebarger, Nathan, Carl and Carla watch construction

together. The boy's dealing with a lot of anger." John would spend time with that boy, and sure enough, he would end up being one of our best.

During those days, we were packing out our first little worship center in two services, and we really needed more space. In 1980 we started our Together We Build capital fundraiser. The building we had designed was a big box with the pulpit in one corner and the seating in four sections fan shaped around in a quarter circle. The ceiling was high, and the north wall was not loadbearing. It was made to be removed so that in the future the building could be doubled to the north, and instead of being a quarter circle, it could swing around and become a half circle.

When the building was just a shell, I walked through it with Russell Sommers, an older man in the church whom I looked up to. Russell was from western Nebraska and had grown up on ranch. He and his wife, Ruby, had come to our church when we were meeting in the Y building and had been with us all these years. Russell and I came in the front door and stepped by the construction equipment.

I looked at him anxiously. He stood there, and his eyes scanned floor to ceiling then left to right. He had his hand in his pocket jingling his change, as he was known to do, and didn't say anything. After a long pause, he said, "You could put a lot of hay in this barn."

Auditorium construction complete

I liked that image, so I began to refer to it as a barn. Over the years as we worshipped there, I oftentimes went over at night to be alone and pray. I called it a glory barn in my prayers: "Lord, may this be a glory barn for You. May this barn be filled with Your glory, and when we gather to meet, be with us in a very special way. Make this place miraculous so that people may be ushered into Your presence here."

As I look back on these years of ministry, they feel like those middle miles of a marathon. In those miles I feel good and look around to see all my training and prep paying off. Likewise, those years of ministry were full of momentum and energy. The church was growing. My family was growing and lending new purpose to the race. But no race is without it's challenges, and there were challenges ahead that I may not have taken on without the wellbeing of my children to consider.

My children were nearing school age, and I wanted them to have a solid Christian education. I wanted them to learn the Bible and be influenced by teachers who loved and served God. I saw the same need among my congregation and responded by opening a school as a mission of our church. In 1980 we started Parkview Christian School with sixty students. I could not have foreseen the struggle into which this decision would plunge the church and my family.

UNEXPECTED VICTORY:
FIGHTING FOR RELIGIOUS FREEDOM
1980–1982

2006 | John helps Carl BQ at WhistleStop

7

ASHLAND, WISCONSIN, October 14, 2006. Hundreds of runners gathered in the tall timber near Iron River, Wisconsin, for the start of the WhistleStop Marathon, which is run on an old railroad bed all the way from Iron River to the quaint, little town of Ashland, Wisconsin. The air was electric with anticipation. All runners know that "It's finally race day" feeling.

It was a cold, crisp morning, not a ray of sunshine—just gray clouds and damp wind swirling through the trees. John, my running partner and brother-in-law, and I were thankful that it wasn't snowing like the day before. The ground, trees, and roofs of the houses were still white, covered with snow. When we ran this race the previous year, the trees were beautiful—gold and red. This time most were bare and stark, having already lost their leaves to the snow-covered ground.

Ten minutes before the start, we got in the long line of runners not too far back from the starting line. As I talked with John, I also went over my mental checklist. I had a few Cliff Bloks in my shorts pockets. In the pockets of my jacket, I had hard candy and sunglasses. I was optimistic about sunshine later in the race. I peeled out of my long pants, though John left his on. I wanted to run barelegged, cold or no cold. My poor legs had enough to carry. I reached down and put my chip on my shoe. Little did I know how significant that little piece of technology would be as I prepared for my ninth marathon.

For me this wasn't just another marathon, this was my shot at Boston. While most marathons are open to whoever pays the registration and is crazy enough to run 26.2 miles, Boston is only open to those who qualify. Making Boston is a goal for serious marathoners and lends them an air of legitimacy.

A guy with a speaker horn tried to give us final instructions, but I could hardly hear over the chatter of the runners—something about two minutes until the start. I was excited; this was what I'd trained for all year. I'd run 105 times, 894 miles, all for this morning and a chance to make Boston. Finally, a foghorn blew, and we were running.

In my quest to make Boston, I had done Chicago in 4:15, North Olympic in 4:11, Chicago again in 4:04, Grandma's in 4:07, and Fort Collins in 4:05. Then in October 2005, John, who runs his marathons a half hour faster than I, agreed to do WhistleStop with me at my pace to help me get that elusive four hour time. We were within two blocks of the finish when my right calf locked up in an unbearable cramp. I staggered in at 4:01:44, excited to get a PR but disappointed that I missed that elusive sub-four. I was determined that this would be the race. I had to make my goal of a four hour marathon to qualify for Boston.

After that southward first mile, we made the turn to the east onto the old railroad bed—25.2 miles to Ashland. A tail wind out of the west was helpful and appreciated. The old railroad bed surface was good, not too soft or muddy, as I feared it might be. It is one reason I like this marathon; the crushed limestone rock surface is easier on the legs.

John and I talked some, but we also just ran along in silence, taking it all in. The northern woods were beautiful even if they weren't as colorful as I'd seen them in the past. Now and then the woods opened up to let us see well-kept dairy farms with their big barns. Runners were as far as I could see in front of me and behind me—maybe 1,000 or more—a lot of crazy people! You had to love it.

WhistleStop Marathon has to be one of the most spectator-friendly races in the world—another reason it's one of my favorites, since I depend on a brilliant, one-woman pit crew. Gayle has come to every race I've run, and I count on her. The old railroad bed that is the running trail runs parallel to Highway 2, allowing spectators to almost follow the runners. When John and I reached mile marker four, Gayle and Marlene, my sis and John's wife, were there, cheering for us and taking pictures.

We saw them again at mile six. The miles were clicking by—ten, eleven, twelve, and halfway, 13.1. We were right on schedule: two hours. I feared cramps and pain in my calves in those latter miles, so I tried not to push it too hard at the midway point.

We passed miles eighteen, nineteen, and finally mile twenty, and our time was three hours and one minute. I hoped that I saved enough strength for those last 6.2 miles.

The course for the race is, for the most part, flat and fast, but there is a slight but long incline here after mile twenty. By this time it seemed like a mountain to me. Every so often a pain shot up my left calf. John was running about eight to ten yards ahead of me. Our plan was for him to keep pace no matter what and not wait for me. The sun broke through the clouds. It was good to see blue sky.

John was twenty-five to thirty yards ahead of me. My left calf hurt. I was afraid it would lock up as my right one had the year before. I tried to push off more with my right leg and limp that left leg forward. Maybe if I could favor it some, it wouldn't cramp. My quads felt good, and I was glad I could depend on them to pull me up this forever incline.

My mile time for twenty-one was 9:20. Mile twenty-two was 9:10. Finally, at twenty-three, I saw Gayle and Marlene. Their encouragement and an aid station kept me going. I grabbed a cup of Powerade and walked through the station drinking it. It was tough to get going again. My body said, "No," but my mind said, "Go!" I could see John a couple of blocks ahead and was determined to keep him in sight.

At mile twenty-four, I reached the end of the railroad trail, and by mile twenty-five turned into Ashland. A security guy watching traffic at the intersection told me, "One more mile to go." I looked at my watch—my total time so far was 3:52. Could I do this last mile in eight minutes? No way! But I decided to give it all I had.

Another race volunteer yelled, "Only ten more blocks to the finish!" I thought, *If you knew how I feel, you wouldn't use the word 'only.'* Ten blocks seemed like ten miles, but I said to myself, *OK, I'm going to count the blocks off. One block, then two, but, oh, the pain!* At least my legs weren't cramping. If I could keep from cramping, I could run with the pain.

Dean Karnazes wrote, "The highest form of competition is self-competition."[1] The battle I was fighting at that moment was not with other runners at all; it was a battle within me. The fight between fatigue and determination was fierce! Fatigue was using its favorite weapon against me—pain. Every step was agony, and every few steps a pain shot up my left calf like an electric shock. I wasn't sure whether it was sweat running down my face or tears.

Then determination countered the pain of fatigue with goals. I remembered the goals I had written down in my dream notebook and reviewed day after day during training. I reminded myself that I had run almost 900 miles in training for this and everybody at home was praying: my family and my congregation. Scripture verses came to mind, like Hebrews 12:1: "Run with endurance the race."[2] I Corinthians 9:24: "Run in such a way that you may win."[3] Philippians 4:13: "I can do all things through Christ."[4] I told myself to focus and finish strong through these last blocks. Run through the pain. Remember what Karnazes said, "Yes, it hurts, but it is a good hurt."[5]

Blocks three, four, five—I quit counting because the crowd on both sides of the street was cheering. What a wonderful distraction. I felt an adrenalin rush, an emotional lift, as I could see the finish line just blocks ahead! John and Marlene would be there and my number one cheerleader, my Gayle, would be waiting for me.

Finally, only a block to go. Marlene was out in the street yelling, "Go, Carl, go!" Through my blurry eyes, I could see the digital clock above the finish line. I thought it read 4:01:20. If that was so, I missed my dream of Boston, but I poured it on, swinging my arms and pumping my legs.

A race volunteer greeted me as I crossed the finish line. He directed me to someone who took the timing chip off my shoe.

Another volunteer put my medal over my head. As soon as I came out of the finish chute, there was Gayle.

The wind was chilly on my sweaty body. She helped me into my big raincoat. We went right by the food tent with its cookies, doughnut holes, and bananas on to the next tent to find the official time. The computer gave us a printed copy of my time: 4:01:26. I felt sick—not only did I feel terrible physically, but my emotions hit rock bottom. I missed Boston! I staggered sick to the porta-potty.

We made our way into the community center to get out of the cold wind. Gayle left me sitting on the bleachers to go look for John and Marlene. As I sat there watching other runners with their families, waves of discouragement and depression came over me. *I gave it all I had. I can't give anymore. Will I ever make Boston? Maybe it's not for me. All those weeks and months of training, strict dieting, and I didn't make it. I thought I could do it. I let everybody down.*

Then Gayle and Marlene came bounding up to me. They were oozing excitement. Gayle said, "You made it! You made it!" Holding my computer printout, she told me how John explained that while 4:01:26 was my clock time. My chip time, which represents the time from when I crossed the starting line to the finish line, was 4:00:58. I made it with a second to spare.

The Boston Athletic Association considered anything under 4:01 as four. As long as the clock didn't click 4:01, you were in, so 4:00:59 was still good. Therefore, my 4:00:58 was good—good with a second to spare! What elation I felt. A victory that I thought was just out of reach was reality. I made Boston!

Those victories that come after near despair may be sweeter than the easy or expected victories. I think that sweetness comes from the value placed on a hard won victory. You know what it took. You know how unlikely it was. Our church has faced these David and Goliath challenges more than once but one stands out as a truly unexpected victory.

On a beautiful day in 1982, I came out of the nation's Capitol and walked down the sidewalk in Washington, D.C. I looked back over my shoulder at the Capitol building. I looked down the mall and saw the Washington Monument and beyond that, the Lincoln Memorial. I was only a couple of blocks from Pennsylvania Avenue on my way back to the hotel.

As I walked into the hotel lobby, the folks at the front desk caught me with the message, "Call your church immediately." I wondered what the urgency was, so I went straight to a pay phone in the lobby and dialed the church's number. I didn't even go up to my room.

Two years before when we started our school, we made an appointment with the Nebraska Department of Education to discuss the issue of licensure. Nebraska law stated that any school that wanted to operate in Nebraska had to have a state license to do so. A church down the road about fifty miles had been battling the state over licensure since 1977 on the grounds that it was a violation of religious freedom. They had gone to court. It was pretty sloppily handled and they lost. Since then Nebraska had taken legal action against numerous church schools and home schools for not being licensed to operate in the state. We agreed with many of these schools in principle but not necessarily in practice, and we hoped we could find a way to settle the issue without conflict.

Pastor Winebarger, our school administrator, Russell Sommers, our deacon chairman and a retired public school superintendent, and I made an appointment with the Nebraska Department of Education. At the meeting, everyone greeted Russell. They knew him since he had been a public school superintendent. We explained to the members of the Department of Education that we would be happy to cooperate with them in any way we could. They could come visit our school anytime they would like. We would use standardized testing to ensure our kids were as well educated as those in the public schools. We hoped for a good relationship with the state. We also explained to them that we were a church, Parkview was a ministry of our church, and we could not fill out an application for a license to operate a ministry of our church. We could not submit our Monday through Friday school to licensure by the state anymore than we could our Sunday school.

For us it was a matter of religious freedom. In this country, we believe it is important that religious practices not be dictated by the state so people are free to worship without fear of government control. When governments or agencies license you, they have the power to un-license you. If the state licenses a school, the state gets to decide what should be taught in the school. It's not just a measure of the quality of education; it's a matter of content. We wanted to be free to teach our children according to our conscience and our beliefs. That didn't mean we intended to shirk our educational responsibilities as the law implied. Instead it meant that we wanted to have Bible classes as well as all the other basic components of an education. We wanted to give our kids a foundation of knowledge and spiritual practice. We agreed to use standardized testing to verify the level of education our students were receiving, and we invited regular visits from the Department of Education. We believed that if state licensure could be given as a seal of quality rather than a permit to operate, we would be more than willing to pursue it. We presented our thoughts to the Department of Education and hoped for a positive outcome.

Shortly after our meeting with the Department of Education, I made an appointment to see State Attorney General Paul Douglas. I wanted to find a solution to this issue. I shared our concerns and told him we wanted to meet the state's standards regarding quality education, but we felt there was a better way than licensure. Though I had spoken respectfully, Mr. Douglas, who was in charge of enforcing the laws of our state, became very angry with me. He shook his finger at me and raised his voice, "You ministers, you think you can pick and choose which laws you like to obey and which laws you don't!"

Finally, I stood. "Sir, I think I should excuse myself and thank you for your time." I left with little hope that the issue could be settled without conflict.

Several pastors in the state organized a group called "Nebraskan's for Religious Freedom," NERF, and asked me to be the director. We lobbied senators with the goal of changing the requirements of the licensure law. We basically had an office in the corner of the Capital near Senator DeCamp's office. Morning after morning we would meet there and make assignments to talk to senators. I was so naive at that time about politics. I honestly believed that if you could sit down with a senator and convince him or her of your position, you could get his or her vote. I didn't understand that often senators were "owned"; they were "bought and paid for." We were up against the largest union in the state of Nebraska, the teacher's union. Nebraska State Education Association (NSEA) put thousands of dollars into senators' campaigns. When senators had that kind of money to help them get elected, you weren't about to get their vote, no matter how convincing you were.

Two weeks prior to being in Washington, D.C., I had an interview with the Lincoln paper, the *Journal Star*, which wasn't uncommon.

We were asked to do a lot of interviews at that time. I came over to my office on a Monday morning. Since it was my day off, I had my son, Nathan, with me. He was two years old at the time. I assumed they were just coming for an interview but they also had a photographer. While I

Front page picture of Carl and Nathan

was talking, they were flashing pictures of us. I never really thought too much about it, and the story didn't come out immediately in the paper.

Now here I was in Washington where I had just met with Mr. Bill Hopner, the aid to Senator Exon. I had been over to the U.S. Department of Education and talked with people there and was back at my hotel with an urgent message to call home.

"Where have you been?" Pastor Winebarger's typically calm voice was tense. He said, "The State has moved on us. Your picture with Nathan is on the front page of the paper. There must be at least a dozen reporters here at the church, and they will not believe me that you are out of state. They are serving papers on all of our teachers and all of our deacons. If that's not enough, the bond company has already contacted us and said they would not process our bonds or take care of our bond campaign."

My heart sank. The church had started the Together We Build campaign and was saving toward the new worship center. We had just dug a huge hole for the basement and were about to sell bonds to build the building. It rained a lot that spring, and we joked about

Jerry Bickert, General Foreman Auditorium

having a big swimming hole. At that moment I thought, *Maybe all we will have is a great big swimming hole.* I realized that the battle had come to our front door.

I called the bond company and persuaded them to continue with the bond campaign. They would only do so on the condition that the prospectus would say that the church was being taken to court by the state for having a school operating outside the law. When they told me they would have to put that in the prospectus, I realized we would not sell one bond outside of our church, and we didn't. Our people rallied and bought all the bonds, thousands of dollars, so we could build the building.

When I came home from Washington, D.C., the first thing I did was call Dr. Elmer Towns at Liberty University where I had taught. I said, "Dr. Towns, would you do something for me? Would you call Jerry Falwell and ask him to get in touch with Mr. William Ball of Harrisburg, Pennsylvania? I want the best attorney in America." I had been following Mr. Ball. I knew if we had to go to court, we wanted the best. He had argued numerous cases before the United States Supreme Court. I knew he was the attorney we needed. Somebody needed to get an outstanding attorney on the scene here in Nebraska and win.

Then came the voice on the other end of the line: "No, I won't do that." My heart dropped, but he continued, "I will give you Jerry Falwell's private number. You call and tell him."

I called Jerry Falwell and told him that we were being taken to court. He remembered me from my time at Liberty nine years earlier, and he said he would contact Mr. Ball and ask him to take our case. We waited and prayed for two weeks for Mr. Ball's decision.

Eventually, Mr. Ball flew out to talk to me. He was a very distinguished man with white hair, a very sharp individual, rather intimidating to me. He spent time talking with us and agreed to take our case. So we fought the battle on two fronts. First, we fought through litigation in the courts, trying to defend our position on licensure. Second, we fought through politics, trying to go through the legislature to change the law.

Across Nebraska the situation was escalating, and several pastors were arrested. Parents were thrown in jail for sending their children to Christian schools. In Gering, Nebraska, summary judgment was granted against the Church of Christ and their school. They were found in contempt of court and fined $100 a day. The school principal was also fined. The church there closed the school, and the people began bussing their children across state lines into Wyoming, so they might teach their children according to their conscience.

Another pastor of an independent church was found in contempt of court because of a summary judgment against his school, and the church was fined $100 a day. He was fined $50 a day. The people of that church also bussed their children across the state line into Wyoming.

In North Platte a pastor was found in contempt of court and was ordered to pay $200 a day. He was put under house arrest and had to report every school day to the sheriff's office at nine o'clock in the morning and was released from jail at three o'clock in the afternoon. His fines at the end of that school year were over $50,000. He was in danger of having his property confiscated by the state.

A church in York, Nebraska, went underground after their church was ransacked. The police along with the County Superintendent had come in, lined up the children, and taken pictures of them. They had taken files without any kind of warrant. The school began meeting secretly in homes.

The Mennonite school in Beaver Crossing also had summary judgment filed against them. There were ten home schools in Nebraska in court. A church in Hardington, Nebraska, was taken to court, and the whole congregation pulled up root and moved into South Dakota. In Louisville, six fathers were jailed through Thanksgiving and Christmas of 1984, and their wives and children fled the state.

As the situation escalated, Nebraska was gaining national attention. Cal Thomas, nationally known columnist, came to our church and visited with us. Jerry Falwell did mailings to help us, or we would never have made it financially. People in churches all over the country were praying.

We prepared for trial for over a year. Our trial was to be June 1-10, 1983. Pastor Winebarger and I both flew to Harrisburg, Pennsylvania, and Mr. Ball schooled us on how to testify in court. We selected some parents and students who were ready to testify as well. Mr. Ball had expert witnesses from around the country with their schedules cleared for that date. For over year we prepared for that trial at a cost of $50,000.

It was amazing to see Mr. Ball in the courtroom. He was a master. I knew the state could tell they had a tiger by the tail. We were ready on the litigation front, but on May 27, just days before our trial,

Judge McGinn called us for a hearing (one of several hearings we had in that year of preparation for trial). He had often ruled in our favor in previous hearings. In this one, however, he declared us guilty without a trial. He called it summary judgment, which means they had tried a case similar to this one and, therefore, didn't need to try our case. Because of the Louisville, Nebraska, case, the judge preemptively declared us guilty and ordered us to finish the school year but not to open in the fall.

We walked out of the courtroom to at least a dozen reporters. They all gathered around me, asking, "Pastor, what are you going to do in the fall?" I explained to them that we had the utmost respect for Judge McGinn and for the laws of the State of Nebraska, but that as a church, we believed God directed us to start this ministry, and we planned to open our school in the fall.

We did open that fall. It was our fourth year of school. The previous year we had 107 students enrolled. We opened our fourth year with eighty-two students. We had lost a quarter of our student body. Monday was a normal day without incident. When we came to school Tuesday, a deputy was parked on the road.

I went into my office and wondered what would happen. After school had started the deputy drove into the parking lot. The secretary buzzed me and said the officer wanted to see me. He came into my office, sat across the desk from me, and said something that absolutely stunned me, "Pastor, I'm on your side. I'm a born-again Christian. My Pastor, Kurt Layman, stands in the pulpit and supports you."

Only a few months before, Kurt and I had spent an hour together on the phone, and Kurt said, "You just need to obey the law and get a license." I explained to him the importance of the school being a part of the church and told him I did not believe the church or any of its ministries should be licensed by the state. If they could license us, they had the power to un-license us and close us. After we talked for an hour, I didn't know where he stood or how he felt about it. I learned that day from the deputy that Kurt Layman had been supportive of us.

The deputy said, "I was told to come here to verify that you're having school. I've got a camera in the front seat of the car. I am supposed to take pictures of the students, but I just can't make myself do it. I'm supposed to find out for sure if you are having school."

I reached over on my desk and picked up the morning paper and pointed to the headlines, "It says right here we're having school." I knew he needed more than say-so evidence, so I went on, "I could take you down and show you the classes if you would like, but it will scare the students." More than once police had come to our school. One time when I wasn't here, they went to the classrooms, walked right in front of the students, and delivered papers to the teachers. I was determined that would never happen again.

He said, "I don't want to do that, I just need your word you are having school."

I said, "We are having school." And he left.

The litigation front did not look good because of the summary judgment. We had been found guilty without a trial though we had been so hopeful of a successful trial with Mr. Ball. We appealed to the Nebraska Supreme Court, but numerous cases like ours had been appealed around the state, and the Supreme Court hadn't received any of them. I didn't know exactly how God was going to take care of this problem. I knew that even if the Supreme Court received our case, this thing could go on for years, and it was taking a toll on our church.

What about the political front? Governor Thone was our friend. I had spoken with him several times. He came one day unannounced to visit our school. I was out of the state, but when I got back, I called him and said, "I want to thank you for coming to visit our school. Governor, one day we are going to have a great school here."

His response was such an encouragement. "No, no, I've seen it. You already have a great school." We were grateful to have the support of Governor Thone.

In the next election, though, Governor Thone lost by a percentage to Bob Kerrey. Bob Kerrey was endorsed by the NSEA. He had said more than once during the campaign that he would veto any law that would change the situation with the Christian schools. All hope that we should be saved seemed lost.

On the litigation front things didn't look good. On the political front we now had a governor who was opposed to us. It just seemed like there was absolutely no hope.

As the State Chairman of NERF, the media often interviewed me. One morning I went out to the curb with a trashcan when the garbage truck pulled up. The garbage man got out, looked at me, and said, "Every time I turn the T.V. on, you're on there." When I would pay for my gas or go to the barbershop, people had all kinds of questions. It put a lot of pressure on the church. We lost all the momentum we'd had. Over time we lost a third or more of our church.

Time and again after church on Sunday while I was shaking hands with people, a family would tell me it was their last week. They were always kind and said, though they loved me, they couldn't handle the controversy and felt God would have them move on. In spite of the kindness, it was devastating to me.

I kept reminding myself and others that it was a privilege to stand on the front line for religious freedom. That God considered us worthy to stand for the autonomy of the church was to be considered an honor. Thankfully, most of our members and school parents shared the same conviction and stood strong.

We tried to keep it low-key at church during those years. When I preached, I stuck to preaching the Bible and the Lord Jesus Christ. We didn't want to turn church into a political thing. Bob Winebarger was busy teaching in the school and serving as Administrator. I was busy being chairman of Nebraskans For Religious Freedom and trying to pastor a church. In that order, I am sorry to say.

I struggled to balance my responsibilities as pastor with my responsibilities as chairman. It seemed everyone wanted to hear our story, whether they were church-goers and Christians or not, and I was often called away for interviews or meetings. Pastor Winebarger stepped in and carried a great load during those years, and I tried to make it a priority not to be gone too many Sundays.

I did accept Paul Kienel's invitation to speak at the International Christian Education Association Conference, where I shared our story with over 900 Christian school administrators.

I also made several trips to Washington, D.C. for meetings. During one of those trips, I had an appointment to meet with Mr. Terrel Bell, the Secretary of Education. I had been trying to get a meeting with him for some time, and he finally squeezed me in during his lunch hour. Our meeting was scheduled for straight-up noon, and I was told I had ten minutes. When I saw that we were scheduled at noon, I chuckled because my favorite movie is *High Noon*. I love watching Sheriff Will Kane stand courageously when everyone else in town folds.

I was there early, waiting for my appointment. I asked God for wisdom and courage and then was ushered into Mr. Bell's office. He greeted me graciously, but we got right to the point. I showed him a notebook filled with clippings of the story as it had unfolded in Nebraska and quickly gave the highlights of our situation. Mr. Bell leaned forward in his chair and began asking me questions. We talked for forty-five minutes instead of the ten I had been expecting. When he stopped asking questions, I stood and thanked him for giving me his time. I knew he had given me most of his lunch hour.

I also established a relationship with Mr. Bob Sweet who served on the White House staff as a speechwriter for President Ronald Reagan. Apparently, it was his assignment to keep an eye on the situation in Nebraska. He invited me to have lunch with him at the Executive Office Building, which is in the West Wing of the White House.

We were encouraged to know that Washington was aware of our plight, but most of all, our concern was that God would keep His hand on us.

In spite of all the upheaval, Gayle and I tried to keep things as normal as possible at home, which was not easy. There was a lot of pressure as the weeks turned into months, and months then turned into a couple of years.

One night after we put the kids to bed, my wife heard our oldest daughter, who was in second grade at the time, crying. She went to her bedside, and through her tears Carey said, "Momma, I don't want Daddy to go to jail."

Then, we noticed that Carla, who was in kindergarten at the time, would get a stomachache whenever she'd eat something. My parents noticed it also and mentioned it. One night after we put the kids to bed, Carla slipped out of bed and came downstairs. I said, "Carla, honey, you've got to go to sleep. You have school tomorrow. You need to stay in bed." But I held her for awhile. We were rocking in the living room and weren't talking about the school issue at all.

All of a sudden out of the quietness she spoke, "Daddy, who would Carey, Nathan, and I go to live with if we can't live with you and Momma anymore?"

I looked across the room at Gayle, our eyes met, and right away we knew what the trouble was. I said to her, "Honey, Jesus is going to take care of us."

As the battle drug on, it seemed there was so little hope in both the legal and the political arenas, and we just couldn't see the light at the end of the tunnel. We had built a building, and we had to pay back the bonds that we were so fortunate to be able to sell. We had lost a lot of students out of our school. Financially the school was struggling, which put a strain on the church finances as well. Things seemed to be going from bad to worse. I would often wake up at three o'clock in the morning and go downstairs and sit in the living room. I didn't even bother to turn on the light. I would pray and remind the Lord what I had told Carla, that Jesus would take care of us.

Finally, we got a call from Mr. Ball, our attorney. The State Supreme Court had made two decisions. First, they received our case. We were shocked because they had refused all other appeals. Second, they gave us a stay to operate until they heard our appeal.

Pastor Winebarger went to tell the classes our school was going to stay open. When he told the first and second grade class, the kids started cheering and carrying on like their team had won the game. The teacher told him that four or five times a day the class would ask to stop and pray that our school would stay open. Before they would go out for recess, they would stop and pray. When they ate lunch, they would pray. After the class quieted down, they asked Pastor Winebarger, "Can we thank God?" The class prayed and thanked God.

We were worn out, but we were never without support. On one of my trips to Lynchburg, Virginia, I was speaking to Elmer Towns and told him I was overwhelmed trying to pastor a church and head up NERF.

He told me about a young couple he believed could help. I drove across Lynchburg to their place and met Todd and Katie Holt[6] for the first time. I was struck by a couple of things in talking with them. I noticed how young and how sharp they were. Todd came to help us with NERF and the church. It was such an encouragement to have them.

We were surprised and humbled by the support we received from around the country. Day after day big trays of letters arrived: letters from school children, letters from churches, more than I could ever begin to answer from people telling us they were praying for us. Often a letter would have a check in it. Twice we received checks for $10,000 to help cover our litigation cost, which was over $100,000 before it was all done. We were very aware that people all over America were praying for us.

One Sunday morning my phone rang. I picked it up, and a guy with a Texas drawl said, "Are you ready to preach for freedom this morning?" Even though he didn't identify himself, I knew it was Lester Roloff. I never dreamed I would talk to Lester Roloff. When I was a kid, my mom used to listen to him on the radio, and I'd think, *Who is that hick preacher?* He let me know he was praying for me.

Several times our phone rang at home, and Jerry Falwell was

calling just to talk to me. He would say, "Carl, how are you holding up? How are you doing?" The encouragement of these guys meant the world to me.

The situation continued to draw national attention. I would come to the office in the morning and find messages from *The New York Times* or the *Chicago Tribune*. People all over the country were wondering, *What in the world is going on in Nebraska?* As I said, Bob Kerrey was elected governor, and we felt that there was no hope in the political realm. Unexpectedly, perhaps because of the nationwide attention, Governor Kerrey appointed a task force of four people to study the Christian school situation: Mr. Bob Spire, the former president of the State Bar Association; Mr. Richard Shugrue, a law professor at Creighton; Mr. Alcurtis Robinson, the vice president of Mutual of Omaha; and Sally Knudsen, a retired public school teacher.

I knew they would be calling me before long, and sure enough, one day they called. Mr. Spire said, "May we come visit your school next Tuesday at eleven o'clock?"

I said, "Mr. Spire, we'd be honored to have you visit our school. After your visit, may we take you and the panel to lunch?" I didn't want them to just do a quick walk-through and leave. I wanted the chance to explain our position and the goals we had for our school and our students.

He said, "Oh, we'd like that!"

We were excited to have the opportunity to meet with them. I called the vice president of the American Association of Christian Schools in Florida and he flew up to attend the meeting and give a perspective on Christian education in other states. We invited a historian from Michigan to come and talk about the importance of the autonomy of the church based on the principle of separation of church and state. We assembled a team of experts and did our best to prepare.

Boy, was it tense around the church leading up to eleven o'clock that Tuesday. When they came, we sat around the table, introduced our guests, met the panel, and shared some coffee and conversation. Then we showed them the school. We took them to the classrooms. I was afraid they would just do a quick walk through, but they didn't. They stood in the back of the classrooms for the longest time and listened to the teachers. They looked at the books. They saw the children raise their hands and stand beside their desks to recite when they were called on. They were impressed.

After the tour of the school, we took them to lunch. I thought that the public school teacher would be against us, but over lunch she said to me, "That's the way it used to be in the public schools when I started teaching years ago." I could tell by the conversation that we were making real headway with this panel. I felt encouraged but hesitant about getting too hopeful.

We waited two weeks, and finally the story came out in the front page of the paper. The governor's task force, his own panel, said the state licensure law was a violation of our religious freedom, and strongly suggested that the law be changed. I obtained the thirty-nine page report from the panel. They said that the issue should be solved and solved immediately. I couldn't have been happier. It was the first glimmer of hope we'd had.

It was a turning point and an answer to prayer! The governor, who was supported by the teacher's union, had appointed this panel, and they had come out on our side. We told them we would submit our children to national standardized tests. They said that was all that was needed. They affirmed that the state had a right to see that children are educated, but they stated that it must do so in the least intrusive way and could not be excessively entangled in the church's ministry. We then waited to find out what the governor would do. We asked people all over this country to pray and write the governor.

Two weeks went by, and one day my phone rang at home. When I answered, a man said, "This is Bob Kerrey." He didn't bother to say Governor Kerrey, and it wasn't a secretary saying, "Wait for the governor, please," just "This is Bob Kerrey." I about said, "Bob who?" He said, "Carl, I've called to tell you I've changed my mind. We're going to get a bill through this legislature, and we are going to change this law. Oh, and please tell people I don't need any more letters about this."

If you had told me a few months before that Governor Kerrey would come to support our cause, I would have called you crazy. But Proverbs 21:1 says, "The heart of the king is in the hand of the Lord . . . He turns it."[7] You'll never convince me that God didn't turn the heart of the governor in answer to the prayers of people all over this state and all over this great country. Little boys and girls in classrooms, mothers and daddies—people all over were praying, and God turned the heart of our governor.

After that, Governor Kerrey would have Bob Spire and half-a-dozen senators come for lunch at the Governor's Mansion. Mr. Spire would talk to the senators, and we started picking up votes we could never get before. A bill passed that spring of 1984, the bill under which we now operate, giving us freedom to operate without a government permit. Today there are thousands of home-schoolers and many Christian schools in the state.

The story doesn't end there, though. You remember Attorney General Paul Douglas who was so adamantly opposed to us, who just about ran me out of his office? He told me that I picked and chose the laws I wanted to obey. A few months after the bill passed, there was a bank failure in our city. The Commonwealth Bank collapsed. In the investigation of that bank failure, it was discovered that State Attorney General Paul Douglas had his hand in the cookie jar all along. He was making thousands of dollars off that bank. The state legislature moved to impeach him. Lest he be impeached, he resigned in disgrace.

Because of Douglas's resignation, Governor Bob Kerrey, who was a Democrat, had to appoint a new state attorney general. Whom did he appoint? None other than Mr. Bob Spire, a Republican, the head of the task force that solved our case and our friend. Mr. Spire and his wife attended Sunday school and church at Calvary twice. He called me several times and visited with me on the phone. Now the governor had appointed him as the new state attorney general in charge of enforcing the laws of this state.

A few years after the school issue was settled, our church celebrated its fifteenth anniversary, and the congregation sent our family to Disney World. What a wonderful experience and a sweet expression of love on our people's part.

One Sunday while we were in Florida, we attended a nearby church. We walked in before the service, and the pastor came over and met us. I told him that I was a pastor of a church in Lincoln, Nebraska. He said, "You have a school?"

"Yes, sir," I replied.

He gasped, "Are you *the* school'?"

I said, "Yes, sir."

The guy about went ballistic. When church started, he asked us to stand and told the congregation, "Folks, these are the people we were praying for."

I thought to myself, *How many pastors and how many churches that we don't even know about and will never meet lifted us in prayer in those difficult days?* We serve a great prayer-hearing God. I can't overstress it.

My life verse became meaningful to me in a new way, "But thanks be to God, who gives us the victory through our Lord Jesus Christ."[8] When victory was out of our reach, God gave it to us. How sweet and humbling. The sweetness of it came from knowing it was shared with people all over America who were praying.

Parkview Christian School stands today as a symbol of the power of prayer. So many kids, including my own, have been taught and ministered to there. One of my grandsons goes there now, and it's making a difference in his life. I'm so grateful for the prayers and support of so many that contributed to that unexpected victory.

SURPRISING SACRIFICE:
GOD PROVIDES IN UNEXPECTED WAYS | 1983–1990

1988 | Answer to Prayer Home
Carl and Gayle with Carla, Nathan, and Carey

8

GRAND ISLAND, NEBRASKA, September 10, 2010. My oldest daughter, Carey, started training for a half-marathon and asked me to run her first race with her. We had fun doing some of our training together and went to Grand Island, Nebraska, to race.

Carey is very competitive, and I knew she would have some speed. As we waited for the start, she told me, "Dad, I'm not gonna push it for my first race, so if you want take off and run a faster pace, go ahead." I wasn't going to leave her, but I told her I'd remember that.

We took off and did the first mile in about eight minutes and forty seconds. We were really trucking. I was sure we'd need to slow down a little bit, but she never did. Every mile was on pace.

It was an out and back course, and on the way back, we were clipping them off passing people. We got to mile twelve and I said,

"Okay, Carey, now kick it in real high gear, and let's finish as hard as we can." She said, "Dad, I'm already there." She told me to go ahead, but I stayed with her. We finished in 1:54.

After the race, we were standing around with the other runners, resting and rehydrating. Race

Grand Island Half Marathon
Carey & Carl finishing strong

organizers started announcing the awards. When they got to my age bracket, they started at third place. I was barely paying attention, but then I heard my name. I was shocked as they announced me as first place in the old guys age bracket.

Sometime later we were down in Dallas to see family, and Carey and I ran the Fort Worth Half-Marathon. This time as we crossed mile twelve, Carey had the extra gear. It was all I could do stay with her. She actually finished a couple steps ahead of me. We both got second place in our age brackets.

She's been after me ever since to run half marathons with her. So far I have been successful in avoiding her, because I know she's getting faster and I'm getting slower. My son, Nathan, ran her last half with her. He's the kind of natural athlete who hardly needs to train. I think I'll let him keep up with her.

That said, it seems I place in half-marathons and am always surprised when I do. I tend to run them for other people, and they end up paying off for me.

VALPARAISO, NEBRASKA, October 13, 2012. A young lady in our church also asked me if I'd run her first half-marathon with her. Michelle had been a volleyball player for the University of Nebraska—a wonderful athlete. Now married with two kids, she missed the thrill of competition and started running. We signed up for a half in the town of Valparaiso, not far from Lincoln, on a trail I often use for training.

We did a couple of training runs together, and I realized she had amazing speed and potential. Then two weeks before the race, Michelle found out she was pregnant. Her doctor said she could run, but he would prefer she kept her heart rate between 120 and 140. Although she was thrilled to have a baby on the way, Michelle was disappointed about not being able to give it her all when she had worked hard to train.

On race day we wore our heart monitors, and whenever our heart rates got close to 140, we would back off and walk. We ran/walked that half-marathon and had a lot of fun, talking and enjoying the beautiful morning.

When we came across the finish line, probably 90% of the people had already finished ahead of us, but the crowd gave us a great round of applause and cheered for us. We finished in well over two and half hours. I teased Michelle that she got first place in her division, the pregnant woman division.

Later I told Gayle that I thought if we could have gone all out, I might have placed in my age bracket, because I didn't see many old guys like me. Well, two weeks later we got a certificate in the mail from the Valparaiso Half-Marathon for first place in my age bracket. I had to have been the only one in my age bracket to get first place with that kind of time. There is a real advantage to being old and entering the small races. You have a great shot at first place in your age division.

Life has surprised me like this before. Just when I think I'm sacrificing, I find myself benefiting. One such time was just after the school battle.

General Foreman, Gary Detweiler Family Life Center

The years of the school struggle had taken a lot out of my family and me and put pressure on the church, but the years following brought recovery and blessing. Having felt the confirmation of our school and the importance of supporting families in our church, we decided to go ahead with plans to build a Family Life Center. We had invested in our auditorium that supported our Sunday morning activities, but we wanted a building that would encourage community throughout the week. We wanted a gym for open gym nights and a stage for productions and events. We needed classrooms for classes, small groups, and meetings. We also believed that the Family Life Center could benefit the school, which was growing and starting sports teams. The gym would provide a place for the volleyball and basketball teams to practice and compete.

We spent several years planning and designing the building. We envisioned a large rectangular building with two levels. There would be first and second-floor classrooms. A hall would run down the middle with classrooms on both sides. A full-length, regulation gymnasium ran along beside the classrooms. It had a racquetball court, a stage, and equipment room. In 1985 we began our Building an Enduring Dream campaign.

Talking about money in ministry makes people a bit squeamish. I realize that, but bear with me. This is really a story of how finances are just tools God uses. In my experience giving to God is rarely a sacrifice for the long-term. But asking people to give is a big deal, and Gayle and I wanted to give as much as anyone for a couple of reasons. We wanted to erase any questions of our taking advantage of our people. We wanted to be in community with them in the sacrifices they were making, not profiting off of their giving. We also wanted to see God provide for us. Selfishly, we wanted to experience God's blessing.

We prayed a lot about our commitment to the campaign, and we committed $20,000. (Again, bear with me through these numbers; they have a point in showing God's amazing provision.) Twenty thousand dollars was our annual salary at the time, and of course, this commitment was over and above what we were already giving in tithe. Our monthly commitment to the three-year Building an Enduring Dream campaign was as much as our house payment, and it stretched us.

We were anxious and had several discussions about the wisdom of giving that much. We wondered what we would do when our children grew up and wanted to go to college since we weren't able to put money back toward their education. Gayle and I agreed that we would have to trust God for our needs in the future and step out in faith now to do what we believed was right. I told God that I'd take care of His business and trust Him to take care of mine.

While the church was expanding, our house in the Highlands was bursting at the seams. The girls were almost teenagers and were sharing a small bedroom. About two years into the Building an Enduring Dream campaign, Carey and Carla said to me, "Dad, we would like a house where we can have our own bedrooms."

I told them there was no way we could afford a bigger house and explained our commitment to the Family Life Center. I said, "You know, kids, you'll just have to pray about this."

They did just that. In family prayer, the girls began to pray, "God, provide a house with four bedrooms, so we can each have our own." They surprised me by tacking on, "Lord, help us to have a house where we can have a horse." If you're going to ask God for something big, you might as well go all the way. A horse! They certainly had not run that request by me.

Gayle and I thought we might as well look—you know, help God along a little bit. Every four-bedroom house we looked at was out of our range, and it seemed there was no way we could make that step up.

One day I got a call from a fellow in our church. His name was Tim. I had baptized him, and he had made some wonderful strides in his spiritual life in the year that he and his family had been in our church. They had moved up to Nebraska from Florida to be near his wife's family and had bought a home just north of the church about five miles in the country. It was an old farmhouse. The place used to be Lincoln Dairy, and Tim had bought the house and five acres and the outbuildings that went with it.

When he called, he said, "Pastor Carl, I've been trying to sell my business for the last year so we could stay in Nebraska, but I can't get it sold. I need to move back to Florida. Would you like to buy my house?" He told me he needed $75,000. I couldn't afford that and told him so, but he said, "I'll tell you what, why don't you come out tomorrow at one o'clock, and we'll talk about it."

I didn't even bother telling Gayle about it, because I didn't think anything could come of it. The next day, I went out to Tim's house. He had papers all drawn up and an attorney there and went over it with me, "Here's the deal, I owe $50,000 on the house at the bank. You would need to get a loan for $50,000." He went on, "I've put $25,000 into the house in remodeling." He had done a lot of interior work and put in new oak floors and kitchen cabinets. "Twenty-five thousand would be between you and me. No interest on that. You just pay me $25,000 and get a loan for $50,000."

I said, "Well, I think I could do that."

I went home and told Gayle I'd bought a house.

Now we had to decide what to do with the house in the Highlands. It was a problem, because the Highlands, which would grow to be the largest subdivision in the state of Nebraska, had not yet been annexed by the city. It was a sanitary improvement district (SID) and was being developed. These were the days of double-digit inflation, though, and nobody was buying a house. The SID built all the streets and put in utilities and then went bankrupt. Homeowners in the Highlands were panicking, and every block had for sale signs. People were selling for a loss and moving out.

It was not a good time to sell our house since we would suffer quite a loss on it. Thankfully, the new house was worth more than I was borrowing on it, so I was able to get the $50,000 loan without a down payment. This allowed us to keep the house in the Highlands and rent it out.

We moved into the farmhouse. It had a bedroom at every corner upstairs, so God answered the kids' prayers as they each had their own bedroom. We lived in the house a few months, and one Saturday morning the doorbell rang. I went to the door and there was a fella'

I'd never seen before. Behind him was a pickup with a horse trailer attached to it.

He said, "I'm here to deliver your horse."

"I'm sorry. You have the wrong place. We didn't order a horse."

He asked, "Are you Carl Godwin?"

"Yes, sir," I replied.

"Then I'm here to deliver your horse."

Carl and our answer to prayer horse

Somebody in the church had found out that our girls had been earnestly praying for a horse, and they bought one and had it delivered to us. The kids were thrilled, but I was a bit baffled. What do you do with a horse when you've never had one in your life? We had a lot of learning to do. We put up electric fence and found a second-hand saddle. That horse became a part of our lives, and you will never convince the kids that God didn't hear and answer their prayers.

When we had lived in the house a couple years, Tim, up from Florida, came by to see me. He said, "Pastor Carl, you owe me $20,000 at this point." I had been working on that loan and had paid him $5,000. I still owed him $20,000. He went on, "I'll tell you what, I don't want the $20,000. I'm in some litigation over my business in Florida. I have to list some assets and things, and I don't want to involve you in any way."

I was insistent, "I owe you the $20,000, and I'm gonna pay it." He wouldn't hear of it. He wanted it written off.

When he left, I sat and thought for a minute and realized

Honorary Doctorate from Liberty University

$20,000 was exactly the amount we had given over the last three years to the Building an Enduring Dream campaign for the family life center. God gave us our money back. On top of that God allowed us to keep our house in the Highlands, and the rent always paid the mortgage until we paid it off. Once it was paid off, the kids were finishing high school getting ready for college. The rent from that house paid for their educations. We hardly had to borrow to get them through school, and what we did borrow was paid off shortly after they had graduated.

Another surprising blessing came in 1995, when I was shocked to get a letter from Liberty University saying they wanted me to come for graduation and receive an honorary doctorate degree. The letter said I was the first person to go out from Liberty to plant a church, and they wanted to recognize that accomplishment.

Gayle and I flew to Lynchburg and were so excited to meet Rick Warren, who was also receiving an honorary doctorate degree, and his wife, Kay. During the ceremony, I walked out on that platform with the honorees and sat down. I looked around the Vine Center filled with thousands of people—graduates and students and their families. All those people were connected with Liberty University. I thought how far the school had come since the days when it was Lynchburg Baptist College, and I taught in a Sunday school classroom.

As I sat on the platform looking over the crowd, I found Gayle just over to my left seated with Mrs. Towns and Kay Warren. Soon, Jerry called me up and said nice things about me and then gave me the degree. As the crowd was applauding, I turned to sit down, but I looked over and pointed to Gayle. I just stood there for a minute and pointed to Gayle. I couldn't help but recognize my teammate. Jerry turned around and, of course, having the photographic memory that he had, called her by name and said, "Let's have Gayle stand." Gayle stood and got deserved applause.

Luke 6:38 says, "Give, and it will be given to you. They will pour into your lap a good measure—pressed down, shaken together, and running over. For by your standard of measure it will be measured to you in return."[1] I'm always amazed at how God provided our needs and then some. My kids got their horse though there was no way I could have given them that. I thought we'd all have to do without because of the financial sacrifices Gayle and I chose to make. God proved otherwise, confirming again that He sees and cares about the desires of even the smallest of us.

RUN THROUGH THE PAIN:
FACING INTERNAL PROBLEMS
1990–2005

2008 | Boston

9

BOSTON, MASSACHUSETTS, April 21, 2008. As John and I rode the bus to Hopkinton and the start of the Boston Marathon, I felt like I needed to pinch myself to see if I was dreaming. Truly, it was a dream come true to run Boston. It was the third Monday in April, Patriots' Day. This race has been run on Patriots' Day since 1897, when fifteen runners ran the first Boston, and John McDermott won.

Race day dawned a clear April morning. The air was charged with excitement. Bill Rogers, four time winner of the Boston said, "There's something very unique about Boston . . . it's Mecca-like."[1] People come from all over the world to run this race, and I got to run with them. I felt like I was in special company. These runners had qualified to be there and had unique endurance and running abilities.

John and I got off the bus and said goodbye to each other. We weren't able to run together because we were in different starting corrals due to our different qualifying times. John's was faster than mine, so he started the race in a faster pace group.

Soon my pace group was called to the start and off we went. The first miles of the Boston are downhill—a perfect opportunity to make the number one mistake of marathoning, starting too fast and forgetting to pace for the pain that comes around mile twenty.

From the start of the race, I was absolutely astounded at the crowds. It seemed the whole city took the day off. Everybody was there. People were in trees. People were on rooftops. People were looking out the windows of buildings. The crowd was dense.

In those first few miles, I was almost solemn as I thought about the great history of this race. I thought about people like John A. Kelley, who ran fifty-nine Bostons. The course runs by his statue in Newton. I thought about Clarence DeMar, who won seven Bostons, Bill Rogers, Frank Shorter, and then later came the women, Roberta Gibb and Kathleen Sweitzer. Then, of course, there was the Duel in the Sun, perhaps the most memorable battle in marathon history, between Alberto Salazar and Dick Beardsley.

Those first miles went well, and I felt good. Somewhere around mile six or seven I saw my twin sisters Marlene, John's wife, and Mary. As their baby brother, I've always been their pet, and they would have delayed me if they could have with pictures and chatting, but I threw them a kiss and went on my way.

At mile seventeen, I saw Gayle, Carla and her husband, Chris, and little Alice, our granddaughter. They were easy to spot in the crowd as they wore bright orange t-shirts they had made that said

Curb Crew Gayle, Chris, Alice, and Carla

Run, Papa, Run. It was great to see them. Around that same time, I was beginning to feel a shooting pain in my left hamstring. As I went by, I told them that my hamstring was hurting, and I could tell they were concerned.

Two things can keep you from your goal as you run. One is injury and the other is attitude. As in life, a million things can go wrong in a marathon, and when one of those things happens, your mind is the key.

One of the best things about running is that it makes you stronger mentally and teaches you how to think yourself through challenges. Running reminds me that attitude has nothing to do with facts but everything to do with perspective. The facts of endurance running are stark. I get tired. My legs hurt, though I still have miles to go. Instead of dwelling on those facts, I choose to think about how good it will feel when I finish. I think about the good I'm doing for my health. Choosing to focus on positives, which are as true as the stark facts only perhaps harder to see, makes the facts fade.

After I saw my family, the hamstring pull got worse and worse until I was running with a limp. I was reduced to using one and a half legs. I came to the four hills and thought again about the history of this course and those who had run through these familiar communities of Hopkinton, Ashland, Framingham, Natick, Wellesley, Newton, and on into Boston proper. Here I was limping and my attitude went south. This was the race I had looked forward to. I really wanted to do well in this one race—this once-in-a-lifetime race.

Waves of discouragement came over me. I couldn't keep my pace. I was dealing with pain every time I brought my left leg up. I could only shuffle that leg forward. Every step up Heartbreak Hill, the fourth in the series of hills, was a matter of conquering pain. I told myself to take it one step at a time and get to the top of this infamous heartbreaker of a hill.

I had to have an attitude adjustment. Yes, this was the race I'd looked forward to and worked toward for years, and I was utterly disappointed to be limping through it. I couldn't change the fact that I was struggling through Boston with a bad hamstring, but I could change my perspective. I remembered how lucky I was to be there at all, at the most historic race in America. I knew I'd better enjoy this moment, the opportunity to be a part of the 112th running of the Boston Marathon. I told myself I would not get a DNF by my name. I would finish. I wanted that Boston Marathon medal, and I would finish no matter what.

At Wellesley all the lovely college girls were giving out free kisses. I just high-fived them—didn't think they would want to be kissing a sweaty, sixty-year-old man. The crowds were cheering as we went by Boston College.

I was trying to keep moving, but the facts were assaulting me. People were going by me. I felt humiliated and exhausted. Amby Burfoot, who once won the Boston Marathon, said this, "While running at first appears to depend on great physical strength and endurance, it is, in fact, almost entirely dependent on strength of mind. Those who have the will will succeed."[2] I knew that strength of mind was the important thing, and I needed to keep feeding my mind good thoughts. Finishing would be worth it regardless of my time.

| **158**

After the race, John and Marlene, Carl, Gayle, Alice, and Mary

After Heartbreak Hill, the course leveled out, and before long we were heading into downtown. By then, I had figured out how to run on one good leg. Those final miles were an exciting descent into Boston, and I couldn't help but get caught up in the moment and the noise of the crowd. All those cheering people have a way of making you forget you're just another also-ran. Instead you feel like one of the elite athletes, leading the pack to the finish of "The Boston."

The finish of the Boston Marathon is an incredible experience. I'll never forget rounding the corner, turning onto Boylston Street for the final 385 yards of the race. Even though I couldn't finish strong, floods of emotion came over me as I realized I was finishing that great race. What a wonderful experience, crossing the finish line. I knew that I had conquered as they hung that Boston medal over my head, even though this was my worst marathon time yet, almost five hours.

Each year the Greek government supplies wreaths of olive branches to crown the Boston winners. Well, I wouldn't have been more proud of my medal if it had been a Greek olive branch. The pain of this race, this difficult run, will fade. The memories of this wonderful experience will remain forever.

This strange paradox of pain in the midst of a dream come true has happened to me in life too. My dream to start a church and

159

be a pastor had been reality for almost three decades when I went through the most painful years of my life.

For me, staff has been both the most encouraging part of ministry and the most devastating. There were years in the 1990s and early 2000s in which staff struggles nearly broke my spirit. Persistence was a well-learned skill by this point, a habit. Keeping on wasn't really the issue, though the pain was enough to make me feel like quitting. The issue was keeping my attitude up—looking at the facts, without letting them derail me. I had to keep my eyes on the positives. I had to find a vision for myself past the pain. It took all I had.

In the 1990s, a football player from the University of Nebraska came to our church. Mike[3] was from Florida and since he was so far from home and family, we sort of took him in. He often came to our house for Sunday dinner after church. He came out from time to time to ride our horse or to hunt.

In the first game of his junior year, Mike, who played linebacker, took a hit and blew his knee. That ended his playing days, which was devastating to him. We mourned that with him, and Mike and I spent a lot of time talking about these unexpected changes in life.

Mike went back to Florida after college, married his high school sweetheart, Stacy,[4] and felt a call to the ministry. After furthering his education, he became a part of our staff.

The Winebargers, who had served with us for over thirteen years had recently been asked to join the staff at a Christian school in Muncie, Indiana. Bob and Karen were born teachers and well suited for the positions. We supported their decision, but the loss was keenly felt. We needed someone to replace them.

Mike and Stacy were ready at just the right time. Mike was

blessed of God with a lot of abilities and was a great blessing to us for a number of years. He helped us make some important improvements and had so much potential.

During this time, we organized what we call our Prayer Partner team, which has been foundational to our ministry. It is made up of church members, who sign up to go through training and then commit to praying weekly. The men are on rotation to pray with me in groups every Sunday before the service. Throughout the week, all of the Prayer Partners pray for the needs of our people. We invite people in each service to fill out a communication card and write down prayer requests or comments. These requests are sent to our Prayer Partners, who pray for each and every one. Prayer is an important part of how we minister to the needs of our people.

I was often grateful in the following years to have this prayer base as our church went through some major changes. We spent a lot of time as a leadership team discussing our purpose, and came up with a one-liner to define it: Leading people into a growing relationship with Jesus Christ. To do this, we felt we had to make some changes.

Our great concern was reaching our community for Christ. We did a phone survey and found that more than half the people in our city said they would not visit a church with Baptist in the name. Our name Baptist seemed to be a hurdle for people to get over. There were some pretty extremist Baptist churches in the Midwest, and we seemed to be painted with the same brush, though we were not technically affiliated with any denomination. We had chosen to use Baptist in our name to express as nearly as we could the doctrines we held.

In time, the name Baptist became confusing and obscured the fact that we were a totally independent, autonomous, indigenous church. I thought about changing the name for a couple years, at least. I knew it would be risky and difficult. We strategized and prayed and planned for a long time. I met with the leadership and the Prayer Partners and shared my purpose for wanting to make the change.

One excellent question was asked: "If we change to a community church with a generic name how will people know what we believe?" We anticipated this concern and already felt it was time to change how people became a part of our church family. We implemented the ball diamond concept that Rick Warren was using. Our vision was to help people become "home-run" Christians by going around the ball diamond. Each base focused on an aspect of faith we believed to be important.

We still use this structure today. In our first base class, 101, we explain God's plan of salvation and our statement of faith. We ask each person if he/she has trusted Christ and Christ alone for salvation and has a relationship with Him as Savior and discuss church membership. In 201, we focus on maturity. Our 301 class focuses on ministering to others, and 401 teaches evangelism. We have "base coaches" to help new people understand our beliefs and become part of our Calvary team, reaching out to the thousands of people in our city.

Our leaders got excited and caught the vision. Their excitement rippled into the congregation, and the transition could not have gone more smoothly. We changed the name from Bible Baptist Church to Calvary Community Church. Though we ended up losing four families, and I don't take the loss of any family easily, I knew that God was directing this. We were making the right decision and would have a better outreach in the long run.

These were years of great growth and movement in our church. Our buildings and land were paid off, and we were debt-free by

2000. Being debt-free allowed us to begin making some necessary additions to our staff. Mike had become my right hand man, but we still had several areas that needed dedicated attention.

We knew we needed to update our music and have a vibrant creative ministry. Mitch and Leisa Larson came to manage and oversee our music and drama. They are the creative force on our team. Mitch's bubbly personality brings joy to church and worship. Leisa has a degree in drama, and together they coordinate and direct a Christmas musical each year, which is an attraction to the entire city. Several thousand people attend. Leisa has since come on as Director of Women's Ministry as well.

Our youth ministry also needed dedicated attention. We found Steve and Terri Davenport in North Carolina. When I called one of Steve's references, this pastor said, "So you're calling from Nebraska?" He chuckled and told me Steve had never been to Nebraska, but his office was filled with Nebraska football paraphernalia. He was a Husker fan. I just knew he had to be our man. Steve is our in-house theologian, and every now and then his opinions on politics and football leak out. He is a power lifter and has set a world record in amateur power lifting. Along with being youth pastor, he teaches Bible classes and strength training at Parkview.

Pastor John and Barb had received an offer to minister at a home for troubled kids in Iowa. Though we were sad to see them go, we knew the work would be fulfilling for them. Their leaving left big shoes to fill in our children's ministry.

Shane Sundermann came to Calvary with his family when he was just nine years old. He grew up in our church and watched his dad's life change as he became a committed follower of Christ and a valuable lay leader in our church. After graduating from Parkview, Shane went off to college and prepared for the ministry. When John

163 |

left, Shane was ready to start ministry, and we were excited to have him and his wife, Debbie, join our team as Children's Ministers. Shane is also a runner and has turned himself into a very successful marathoner and ultramarathoner.

Mom and Dad had started a Grandpeople's Ministry years before, and when Dad retired, they committed all their time to working with and ministering to the Grandpeople in our church. They were volunteers, but they worked like staff members. Mom would set up the calendar for the year and organize monthly activities. She would take note of who was there or who was missing, and Dad would teach the Grandpeople's class. They loved ministering to that class.

I enjoyed our team; our staff meetings were fun. We met every Tuesday and Friday morning. On Friday mornings, we'd meet at 6:45 for prayer and then go to breakfast together before staff meeting. It gave us a chance to talk football and politics and solve the world's problems before we got down to business.

With added staff, I found there was also added responsibility. I knew these families had needs that must be met, and I felt the burden of their livelihoods. Running became my refuge. They say most runners are running from something. As the load at church got heavier and the ministry got greater, the more necessary my running became. Little did I know how much I would need that refuge. There was great pain ahead—deep valleys to walk through. It seemed like God gave me running to help me to get through difficult days.

Personally these were difficult years. My son, Nathan, made choices I knew would impact the rest of his life. Gayle and I cried and prayed for him. I began to reflect back on the years I had invested in the church and wondered if I had invested enough at home. There were many nights Gayle cried herself to sleep.

Then in 2001, we found out my mom had ovarian cancer, and she began a two-year battle that would eventually take her life. It was difficult to see Mom waste away with cancer and become weaker and weaker as the days went by.

That same year a strange thing began to happen with our staff. We went to a Willow Creek Conference in Chicago. Before we went I talked with the staff and said, "We will be able to use some things from this conference in our church, but we must also remember that we are Calvary Community Church of Lincoln, Nebraska. We are not Willow Creek Church of Chicago. Not everything they do there will fit us here. We need to keep that in mind." Even Pastor Bill Hybals reinforced that at the conference when he said, "You have to discern what works in your ministry."

When we got home from the conference, though, it seemed that Mike wanted us to be like Willow Creek. We had already changed a lot in our church, and I was very pleased with the progress we had made, but Mike wanted more to change. There was a drive to follow the mega church trend. He felt we needed to drop our Wednesday night children's ministry, AWANA, because it was somehow outdated. AWANA is a very effective program, and I wasn't sure it needed to be dropped just because it wasn't the newest and brightest.

Mike kept pushing for that and other changes I just couldn't go along with. He seemed to disregard my input and mocked AWANA to the other staff. I could tell he considered me old fashioned, and maybe he was right about that. I've never felt that just because something is newer it is better, and I couldn't see adopting that

165

attitude now and trying to follow the trends of the mega churches regardless of the cost. I wanted growth as much as the next guy, but I wasn't going to sacrifice the vision we held for our people and our church.

For the first time in the history of our church, we were having problems among our staff. We were having internal problems rather than being attacked from the outside.

This went on for over a year. Our staff meetings, which had been a lot of fun and very profitable, turned icy. Oftentimes Mike would roll his eyes at ideas or suggestions. Though I felt support from the rest of the staff, I knew I was losing touch with Mike, which was hard for me to believe because he had been almost like a son for years. We were close. I was dumbfounded, as it seemed like we were drifting apart. I kept trying to reach out to Mike, but we were not able to get back on the same page. Many nights, I tossed and turned on my pillow trying to figure it out.

After a rough night, I would often get up early, before daylight, and run. I relished my time in solitude, thinking and praying, "Lord, what should I do?" My course was four miles around the square-mile section. Most of eastern Nebraska is divided into square-mile sections. On the far side of the section, just about the two mile mark, there is a hill that I named Victory Hill. When I crest the hill, I'm heading south and can look over the city. I can see the state capital. I always say my life verse, I Corinthians 15:57 and 58, "But thanks be unto God, who gives us the victory through our Lord Jesus Christ. Therefore, my beloved brethren, be steadfast, immovable, always abounding in the work of the Lord, knowing that your toil is not in vain in the Lord."[5] That verse kept me in ministry when I wanted to walk away in the first years of the church. I had committed to staying with this church no matter what. Back then it seemed that might mean setting up folding chairs in a rented building for the rest of my life. That verse had seen me through those early years and the years we walked through the legal battle with the school. Now, I said it from an aching heart as the ministry had become very painful.

I began to dread staff meetings because there was tension in the air. It was spilling over into our leadership meetings with the deacons and into the congregation. Our church had always had a family atmosphere with a lot of love. That was slipping away, and I was burdened by the loss.

In 2002 we had an extended leadership meeting with the staff and the deacons at my house. Prior to this Mike had been talking to me about starting a Saturday night service that he would lead. I was not opposed to it, but I had made it clear to him that I needed to know that he was loyal. I needed to know that if I made a decision he didn't agree with, he would stand by me. To me loyalty means trusting the intentions of a leader so that even if you don't agree with a particular decision you support the leader, as long as there's not a moral issue involved. I felt this loyalty from Mitch and Steve and Shane, but I really wasn't seeing it in Mike. Until I did, I wasn't willing to put the unity of our congregation at risk by taking this step.

At the leadership meeting at our house, we were doing a lot of talking and planning, and one of the deacons brought up starting a Saturday night service. I knew right then that Mike had been talking with the leadership team, trying to build support, and was doing an end run around me. A couple of the other deacons chimed in, and then Mike began talking about how we ought to have a Saturday night service. I knew we had crossed a line. They were trying to force this through, knowing I was not for it. I needed to hit this problem head-on.

167 |

I said to our team, "Guys, we cannot start a Saturday night service and have Mike lead it, because Mike and I are not on the same page." I explained that I loved Mike like a son, that we had served together for years, and that I wanted to continue to do so. I told them that prior to this meeting, I had told Mike we were not going to consider a Saturday night service at this time. I emphasized that the fact that it had come up in this meeting without my being informed it was on the agenda demonstrated the issue. Mike was willing to sacrifice his relationship with me and the wellbeing of our team for the sake of getting his way. It seemed to me that at least four of the eight deacons agreed, but three of them didn't, and one could go either way. Well, the meeting did not end well, and before things got better they got worse.

In 2003 Mom was obviously losing her battle to cancer, and the Lord was preparing her to go Home. Before she went to the hospital the last time, Mom hung a dress on the back of the bedroom door for her funeral. As she was dying, she said to Dad, "I hid some money." She told him where it was in a drawer at home. She had hidden several thousand dollars in small bills to help pay for her funeral.

I was with Mom when the Lord took her Home. Mom had supported me from the beginning. She was there every week. I knew she was proud of me. To lose her was to rip a hole in my purpose. My purpose was ultimately to follow God's calling for my life, but making Mom proud was very important to me and not seeing her there when I preached was an unexplainable loss. Still is.

Also in spring of that year, Mike decided that he was going to leave the staff at Calvary and start a church in Lincoln. I remember the meeting when he told the deacons of his decision and then stood and went out the door. I excused myself from the deacons and walked with him down the hall. As he prepared to leave, I gave him a hug and told him I loved him and wished him the best.

The next Sunday, we announced that my mother had died and that Mike had resigned. It was a jar to the church. Over the next few months, we saw over 150 people leave our church little by little, like cutting a dog's tail off an inch at a time. As a pastor losing anyone from your flock is painful. You feel the rejection and the hurt. You live with the tension of lost relationships, knowing you've been a real disappointment to some people.

Soon a family I never thought we'd lose chose to leave, and I felt rejection in an entirely new way. Todd and Katie, our dear friends of over twenty years, decided to leave with Mike. Todd and Katie had come to help us during the school struggle. When that was over, Todd went into law enforcement and became police officer here in Lincoln. Katie stayed on as the administrative assistant at the church. Assistant is far too small a word for all she did. She was as organized and detailed as I am unorganized and big picture. She was an integral part of the team.

Todd and Katie were not just a part of our team and members of our church, they were our close friends. They were probably, humanly, our greatest source of encouragement. Todd and I were hunting buddies. Our families got together for special occasions, watched football together, spent Thanksgivings together.

That year they told us they had other plans for Thanksgiving, and I could see the handwriting on the wall. It was devastating to Gayle and me to lose our friends. We were crushed and felt the hurt deeply.

Several months after Mom died, Dad and I went turkey hunting. We took a couple days and went north, near the South Dakota line.

He was eighty-five years old and still going hunting, still active and full of life. When we got back in the afternoon, I took dad home. That evening I called to see how he was doing. He said, "I'm so lonesome I could die." I knew that Dad was really struggling without Mom. He had come home to an empty house. There was no one to tell his hunting stories; Mom wasn't there to listen to him.

As the weeks went by and turned into months, I noticed that Dad took an interest in a lady in our church named Betty. Dad and Betty began seeing each other. A year later, I had the joy of uniting them in marriage. They seemed to have a great time together. They traveled and enjoyed each other.

Then as Dad turned eighty-six, we found out he had prostate cancer that had gone into his bones. For a year Dad took all kinds of treatments and fought that cancer, but I saw him slipping away, just as Mom had.

After a year's treatment, Dad had a series of tests. He and Betty and Gayle met with the doctor to hear the test results. Gayle called me and said, "The doctor told us Dad's scan was lit up like a Christmas tree." The cancer was all through his bones. There was no need for more treatment. It was time to call hospice.

I went to see Dad at his and Betty's house. Back in the bedroom, he was sitting up in the bed with pillows behind him. He looked so small propped in the bed, surrounded by Betty's floral décor. Dad had always been a big man, but his body had withered with the cancer. He'd gone from over 200 pounds to 140. I sat in a chair by the bed. He said, "I suppose you heard the report."

"Yes, I did, Dad."

"Well, I'm going Home," he said.

For the next fifteen minutes, we had the most amazing conversation. Never did a tear come to his eye as he said, "I'm going

Home." We talked about Heaven. I opened my Bible and read some scripture. I stood and held his hand, and before I prayed, he said to me, "Now, you go on and build the church." He knew we had talked of expanding the building, but he meant a lot more than the building; he meant the church, the body of believers. He said, "Now, you go on and build the church." For me it was a recommissioning from my dad.

I said a prayer and really wanted to lean over and kiss him on the cheek, but I had a big lump in my throat. I was afraid I would lose it. I didn't want to cry because he did not cry. So I squeezed his hand and said, "Dad, I'll catch you later. I better run."

I got out of that bedroom, and there was Betty across the living room, looking out the glass door to the backyard. She opened her arms to me, and I came over and put my head on her shoulder and sobbed silently.

I drove home, knowing I was going to lose the one who had taught me how to hunt as a little boy and had taught me so many things about life. We started our church in his home, with his support. He had served faithfully all those years, and he was going home to his eternal reward. Through my tears, I strained to see the road as I drove home. When I got there, the only relief I could think of was to go run—to put on my running shoes, take off, and run.

In those days when everything seemed so difficult, nothing brought me joy like running—just me and my dog running along in silence listening for a meadowlark to sing or a rooster pheasant to crow. In the winter going out for a noontime run, bundling in an old hooded sweatshirt and gloves, pulling that string on the sweatshirt so I could hardly see out, just a hole in front for my eyes and nose and mouth, trying to stay warm running in the snow. Or in the summer getting up at 4:30 and hitting the road before the sun is up and watching it get light. Running by farmhouses, seeing the light on in the kitchen, knowing people are just getting up, and feeling like I'm ahead of the game. Then running east on Bluff Road and seeing the barn on the hill and the farm pond, the old schoolhouse with the belt of trees north of it. Then the sun spilling over the eastern horizon. It seemed to me the purest exercise known to man, just running, picking them up and putting them down. Simple. Didn't have to think hard just pick them up and put them down. One foot in front of the other.

One of my mottos is "Bring people up to where your attitude is." It was all I could do to keep my attitude up during those days. Here I was in what should have been the best years of my ministry, running the race of my life, and I was facing my biggest struggle. It seemed like constant pain. Oftentimes I would go to staff meeting and try to be chipper, but inside I was struggling. The facts were hard to get over. I had lost Mike and felt betrayed and uncertain.

Sunday after Sunday, I would go up onto the platform to the pulpit two steps at a time, feeling physically strong. Emotionally, though, I was crawling up those steps on my hands and knees. I felt like I was reaching to the pulpit and pulling myself up, struggling to share a message with people from a very hurting heart.

Those struggles gave me a new empathy for the pain others were feeling, and I did my best to bring my attitude up and put my faith in the Lord and in His precious promises and keep on singing the victory song. I knew in a new way how people were hurting, and in many cases, they were hurting far worse than I was. They didn't need to come to church only to walk out with a heavier heart than they had come in with. During sermons, I made a special effort to tell funny stories or say something to make people laugh.

I'll never forget the time a man who had been attending our church made an appointment and came to see me in my office. He had a litany of things that were wrong with Calvary. One of those things was that I used too much humor in the pulpit. When he said that, I stopped him and said, "You know, I think there's probably a church in town you would feel more comfortable in than you do here at Calvary, because I am not going to stop trying to help people laugh. Proverbs says laughter is medicine. Hurting people need to laugh."

During the struggle with Mike as I tried to find ways to unify our staff, we attended a Promise Keeper's conference. While we were there, I met a man from Oregon, and as we talked, he told me he was a coach to pastors. He gave me a brochure, and I tucked it away.

When Mike resigned and I felt like the world was crashing in around me, I found that brochure. I went to the website and gathered all the information I could. It was a one-year program of coaching over the telephone.

I took it to the deacons to get the funds approved. I told them I felt I could use somebody to talk to and thought that an objective opinion from someone removed from the situation would really help me gain perspective and grow. The deacons, to a man, were 100% for it. I was grateful because inside I was dying. A lot of mornings I wondered how I could make it through another day.

Talking with my coach on the telephone every other week was a great encouragement. I learned a lot and was comforted by the conversations. My coach articulated something I knew inside but hadn't been able to put into words. He said he believed if Mike didn't learn to be a good follower, he could never learn to be a good leader. That concerned me greatly for Mike because I did care. I wished I had been able to say to Mike in a way that he could have understood that my concern about letting him lead had to do with the importance of his learning to follow. Unfortunately my coach was right. Nine years later, Mike's church asked him to leave to deal with personal and family problems. How I wish I had been able to help him.

These years of pain reminded me of the importance of attitude. There was little I could do to change the circumstances. The facts were grim—like limping through Boston—but I realized that attitude is as true as fact. I was still running my dream race. I was still called "Pastor Carl." There was much to celebrate. The pain would pass.

It seemed like it took me most of a year to come out of the tailspin of seeing the church suffer a setback, but as 2005 came, we had begun to shake it and were ready to go. We organized a big year with a lot of plans. I knew vision mattered. To get past these struggles, we needed fresh vision.

2004 | *North Olympic Discovery Marathon*
John, Carl, Chris

10

SEQUIM, WASHINGTON, June 13, 2004. Proverbs 27:17 says, "As iron sharpens iron, so one man sharpens another."[2] No one has sharpened me more in the area of distance running than my brother-in-law John Munson and my nephew Chris Jones.

After doing a couple of marathons, I started talking to John and Chris about running one with me. They agreed, and we signed up for the North Olympic Discovery Marathon, which is run in June in the very northwest corner of our country, north of Seattle, Washington.

Since all three of us were running, we ended up with a bit of a family gathering in Washington. Eighteen of our extended family gathered to watch the race and enjoy the beautiful area. My niece Tammy, Mary's daughter, had signed up to run the half-marathon. Two of my dad's sisters, Daisy and Violet, live out there. They have always been my favorite aunts, and it was great to have an excuse to stay with them.

Most of the family flew out, but Gayle and I thought we would drive and make a vacation of it. For us vacations have usually been road trips. We headed west across Nebraska and up into Wyoming. From there we decided go to Lake Louise and see the Canadian Rockies and Glacier National Park. We spent a couple of nights camping.

One morning when we were taking up camp, I bent over to pull a tent stake, and pain shot up my back like lightning. I knew I was in trouble. I could hardly stand up.

We were at least two days drive from Seattle. Gayle had to drive the whole way. By the time we reached my aunts' house, the pain had intensified. That night I could not sleep. I was really distressed knowing I was a day away from the marathon. I wanted to run it so badly. Family was coming. John and Chris were counting on me for this marathon, and my back was out. I climbed out of bed and lay on the floor, trying to deal with the pain. I prayed about it, "Lord, I really want to run this marathon, and I am in great pain. Help."

I woke Gayle up at six o'clock and told her I thought we should go to the emergency room. I needed some relief. Race or no race, I couldn't handle the pain anymore. Instead, Gayle looked in the Yellow Pages and found a chiropractor. She called the emergency number, and he met us at his office at 6:30 that morning.

I walked into that chiropractor's office like a ninety-year-old. I could barely hobble. Gayle told him that I was scheduled to run a marathon in twenty-four hours, the next morning. I didn't even think it was worthwhile to tell him I was trying to race. I just was hoping I could recover enough to walk. The chiropractor looked at me and grinned, "We'll have him ready by tomorrow morning." I thought he was crazy. How would I run when I could hardly walk? Every step I took was painful, and running seemed out of the question.

But when he said that, it gave me hope. "Look," I said, "If you really think you can get me ready to run, you do whatever you have to. I want to run that race." I almost regretted my words. He worked on me for two hours straight and then told me to go walk for a half hour. After I walked, he worked on me for two more hours, all morning long.

He sent me back to my aunts' house with instructions to ice my back and walk in half hour rotating increments for the rest of the day and to come back to see him in the evening. So that's what I did all day. Iced and walked.

Finally, late in the afternoon I tried to jog. I jogged about ten steps, and the pain was there. I walked some more, tried jogging again, and was able to jog a little.

He worked on me that evening and the following morning and sent me off to the race with instructions to run through the pain for the first mile and then I'd be all right.

I was thrilled as I rushed to the start to meet John and Chris. Waiting for the race to start, we chatted and worked out our nerves by cutting up and teasing each other. I dramatically relayed the story of my back injury and sang the praises of the chiropractor. They teased me about being an old man and making it through the race. They shared their jitters with me. They were about to do something they had never done before. Our spirits were high as we set out.

When the race started, I was so worried their teasing would prove true and my back wouldn't hold up, but the chiropractor was right. I could feel that pain in the lower left of my back, but after a mile, it was gone.

The North Olympic Marathon is very spectator friendly since it's small, only 300 or 400 runners. We had a great curb crew with so much of our family there, and we were able to see them at miles four, eight, thirteen, and sixteen. My twin sisters, Marlene and Mary, were there. Marlene is John's wife and Chris's mother. Chris's wife and family came. My daughter Carla and several others were there too. My eighty-something-year-old aunts even came to watch.

John, Carl, and Chris nearing the finish line

The miles clicked off, and we were enjoying our run. The course goes from the little town of Sequim to Port Angeles right on the Puget Sound. The area is natural and wooded. Part of the course runs right along the Pacific coast. We could look out as we ran and see the ocean. Our pace worked for all three of us, so we stayed together. Company made the miles and hours go by quickly. Before I knew it, we were well past twenty.

Soon we came to mile twenty-five. Chris told me I was going to get a PR and beat my fastest time so far, which was 4:15. He told me to lead and give them a good last mile. By this time my legs were screaming, but I certainly wasn't gonna let them down. I gave it all I had and stepped up to lead us in. Later Chris told me, "I asked you to go a step ahead because I didn't want you to see the tears on my face. I was hurting so badly I was literally crying." The agony of the last miles of a marathon can make a grown man cry.

Carla, Carl, and Gayle

We crossed the finish line in 4:11. I had the joy of that finish-line-feeling again, and this time I got to share it with John and Chris. It was great to see them getting hugs from their wives and families after the race. I loved experiencing the euphoria of their first marathon finish with them.

These guys would push me and sharpen me in the days ahead to help me take my running to another level. Marathoning is not a team sport and yet bonds are forged among runners. John and Chris and I have for a decade now shared a great bond that only runners know.

Our daily lives and personalities are very different. John is an engineer. He's a quiet, detailed, perfectionist kind of guy—opposite of me. I'm a sanguine people-person—big-picture guy. Chris is an attorney, an optimist, and a wonderful father and husband. But we share one passion, running. This passion binds us together, and we spur each other on.

Once they had experienced a marathon, they were not content to just run a few more. They wanted to take our running to another level. They wanted to BQ, Boston Qualify. They would go on and run ultras. In fact, John would run the Leadville fifty-miler up in the mountains of Colorado to the little town of Leadville. His picture would be in the *Ultra Runners* magazine. On every birthday now, Chris runs the forty-two miles from his home in Kansas City to Lawrence, Kansas.

Life, like running, tends to be a solo sport. By that I mean that the struggle is often internal. When you run a marathon, the struggle happens in your mind. Your mind decides if your foot can take another step. You compete with yourself and with your own fears and aches.

Life is like that; so much of the daily work is internal. I have discovered in running and in life that having someone with you to help you with that internal battle can make all the difference. Sometimes a running partner can simply take your mind off the pain. Sometimes they pace you or, as Chris once did for me, literally take you by the hand and drag you the last painful .2 miles. They push you to be more than you think you can be.

The nice thing about running is that the goal is clear. A team can run with unity because there is no question where they're headed— to the finish line. Since the route is preset, there's no debate about how to get there. In life and ministry, of course, this kind of clarity is rare. Nevertheless, I've found that ministering with a team is as vital as it is challenging. Working with people committed to a common cause is a special kind of camaraderie. It builds commitment and unity.

There is no way to carry the load of a church alone and having a team that works matters. I believe it is essential to have people who can help me keep perspective, share the joy, and bear the load. As you reach for your goals, find people who believe in you and share your vision. They can be few and far between, so when you find them, hold onto them.

Through years of ministry, I've learned to look for those people. Building the team at Calvary has been some combination of providence and intention. As a pastor, I want people around me who have the strengths I lack. I know my weaknesses, and I try to find people who fill those gaps to minister with me. For the most part, that has worked. Thankfully, God knows better than I do who will fit. I've often seen His hand in bringing the right person to us at the right time.

Steve, Mitch, and Shane stood by me through all of the struggles with Mike and continue to serve faithfully. When we had made it past those difficult years, I knew we still had areas that needed attention. We added Cleve and Kim Smith to serve on our team as the Adult Ministries and Administrative Pastor. Scott and Karen Wiles took over the Grandpeople's Ministry. Mozart and Colleen Dixon began building our College and Young Adult Ministry and our ministry intern program.

Besides our staff, we've invested in daughter churches. Two of our couples have planted a church in Kentucky, Pastor Doug Tucker and his wife, Angela, and Assistant Pastor Jerry Hansen and his wife, Susan. Doug came to our church as a rowdy young man and ended up committing his life to Christ and ministry.

Greg and Billie Fletcher founded The Master's Chapel in Booneville, Indiana. Greg came to church during his years as a student and football player at the University of Nebraska. He met Billie, an all conference volleyball player for the national championship team at the University, and they married and moved back to her hometown. They couldn't find a church there that preached the Bible so they started one.

Mark and Gayle Schanou have gone out from our church and are planting a church in Grand Rapids, Iowa.

We have always depended heavily on our congregation to volunteer, and they never fail to step up. We are a family at Calvary— not *like* a family, we *are* a family. We never apologize for calling people to sacrifice, serve, and be committed to this great cause—the cause Jesus launched when He said, "I will build my church."[3] Jesus called people to commitment. So many have responded as we have communicated this call to His cause. I could mention enough names to fill pages, so I won't begin such a list. But we have folks who give of their time every week to greet people, organize the Prayer Partners, teach classes, lead small groups, work with children, sing on the worship team, run the sound board and lights, and provide hospitality on Sunday and special services throughout the week.

Of course, our church members who are faithful week by week are an integral part of the daily workings of Calvary Community Church. There are even a few members still active and attending who were there before we had any buildings and were meeting in rented facilities. They have been faithful all these years. My heart is moved every time I see one of them in church. What dedication and commitment they have demonstrated.

I have always had a team of deacons to advise and counsel me. How grateful I am for the leaders God has raised up to make Calvary the outreach it is to our city. I treasure the input of our deacon team. It's a joy to serve our wonderful Lord together.

Most of all, I couldn't manage ministry without my pastoral team. You would think that after a deeply painful staff experience, I would tend to rely on my staff less for fear of experiencing that hurt again. Instead, I find it's the exact opposite. That experience taught me the importance of having outlets outside of church, such as running or attending Ford Car Club meetings and talking classic cars with the guys.

Both of my outlets, running and classic cars, have turned into outreaches and have given me the chance to connect to people who may not share my faith.

About ten years ago, I had the opportunity to buy a 1946 Ford

Carl's 1946 Ford

just like the first car I had in high school years. After we got the ol' car, Gayle and I decided to join the Early Ford V8 Club. We wanted to be around car experts and get to know people outside of our Calvary family.

I remember the first club meeting that Gayle and I attended like it was yesterday. We were a little nervous since we didn't know anyone. We wondered if they would accept a guy who is not a mechanic but just loves old cars and is a preacher, of all things. It didn't take long to find out. They have adopted us as the club's pastor. They ask me to give thanks before any and every meal we have together. Whenever someone from our club is in the hospital, I try to get by to visit.

Now, once a year, Calvary has a special outreach we call Summer's End. On that day after church, we have dinner on the grounds, fun activities for the kids, and a big car show. Our Ford Club helps us make it special by bringing their cars and inviting other clubs. They even come for the service to hear me preach.

They have not only accepted Gayle and me, they've made us feel special. They help me mechanically, and I've tried to help them spiritually. I guess we all have our callings.

It is such a joy when something I love as much as running gives me the chance to get to know someone in a deeper way. One such relationship that stands out to me is my friendship with Michael Tolland. His wife had been attending our church for some time when she came up to me and told me that her husband was coming with her the following week. He was a marathoner and couldn't quite believe that a pastor could be a marathoner too. After attending several for several weeks, Michael asked if we could get together for coffee. Over coffee, I shared with him what I believe about Jesus, and he prayed and began a relationship with Jesus as his Savior.

We logged a lot of miles together during the years he was in the doctoral program at the University of Nebraska. When he finished his degree, he accepted a teaching position at the University of Kentucky. He comes back to run the Lincoln Marathon every year and always makes it to the second service at Calvary after the race.

As I spend time on these other things, I find myself relying on my staff more, and they step up to the challenge. Each is fully responsible for his/her area. We meet regularly to discuss issues and plans, but they carry their own loads. I no longer feel the need to carry it all. It's amazing how much you can accomplish when you do what you can and get others to help you.

STILL RUNNING THE RACE:
THE CHURCH ENDURES | 2005–PRESENT

11

HE CONQUERS WHO ENDURES

—Persuis

ASHLAND, WISCONSIN, October 15, 2011. My run at Boston left me hungry. The race was every bit as thrilling and historic as I had hoped it would be, but a hamstring injury wrecked my pace. My time was nowhere near my potential. Since the Whistlestop Marathon had served me well in my first attempt to qualify for Boston, I decided it was my best chance to qualify again. I talked my nephew Chris into running with me to help me keep my pace. Since I was in the sixty-five to sixty-nine age bracket, I had an additional ten minutes of qualifying time. A 4:10 marathon would get me back to Boston.

That qualifying time had recently been tightened from 4:15. There had been another change to the qualification rules since I last ran for Boston. Before if I made the time, I was in. Now, if I made the time, it didn't mean I was in. It meant I could apply for Boston. They would take the fastest qualifiers from the year of marathon runners who applied.

Chris is Mr. Optimist. He was convinced that not

Going for that sub four with optimistic Chris

only would we get a qualifying time, we would also do a sub four. Chris is some twenty-five years younger than I am and is a natural athlete. He's a very good runner and runs more like seven-minute miles when he does his marathons, two minutes a mile faster than my pace. His goal is to make the Fifty State Club by running a marathon in each of the fifty states. He hadn't done one yet in Wisconsin, so I figured this would help us both. He'd get his Wisconsin marathon, and old Uncle Carl would get a shot at getting back into Boston.

Race morning was cool, and we relished the first miles of the marathon, talking and enjoying the beauty of the Northern Wisconsin woodlands and dairy farms. As we talked, I tried to remember to breathe deeply through my nose and exhale through my mouth to get as much oxygen to my muscles as I could. I didn't want to cramp. I reminded myself the nose is for breathing and the mouth is for eating.

The miles were going by as Chris and I ran along chatting. I felt blessed to run with him. I remember my wife and I babysitting him, trying to get him to eat his scrambled eggs while he sat in his high chair. Now he was helping me pace a marathon. We talked about our passion for running, but we also talked about our passion for Christ. I asked Chris about his spiritual journey. It was a joy to hear him share that the most powerful spiritual influences in his life were his grandpa and grandma—my mom and dad. I wondered just how many lives they had touched for Christ.

As we went by mile twenty, we were right on schedule—three hours, but now the real work began. Marathoners have a well-known saying, "The last six miles are the last half of the race." I knew that Chris was really counting on me to get sub-four. I was picking them up and putting them down the best I could, but I did feel it as we were struggling and getting higher into what I call "thin air."

During miles twenty-two and twenty-three, I was struggling to keep close to a nine-minute pace and not quite making it. Chris was still optimistic, sure we were going to make sub-four. But I wasn't quite keeping pace, and I saw it slipping away as we neared the last mile.

Come on, Carl!

Chris urged me on, but the pain was excruciating. I realized I wasn't going to make sub-four, which made it hard to keep pushing. Finally, we saw it up ahead, mile twenty-six. We were in the city of Ashland. The crowd was cheering. As we crossed mile twenty-six, Chris had, I think, grown impatient with me. He reached over and grabbed my hand and literally began to pull me. We had .2 of a mile to go, 385

191

yards. It was all I could do to keep my legs under me as he pulled me, not letting me ease off or slow down. Chris kept pulling me until we crossed the finish line.

I was exhausted, and I realized we did not make sub-four. Chris's family and Gayle greeted us. We got the computer print out and our official time was 4:01:05. We didn't make the sub-four, but maybe, maybe I made Boston. At least I could apply.

We walked through the food tent for the runners and grabbed a few snacks. As we came out on the other side of the tent, my left leg cramped severely. If it weren't for family to hold me up, I'd have gone down. I had just made it. That had been my problem in the last mile or so of that race. The back of my legs had begun to tighten up. I'm sure Chris wondered why I didn't push harder, but I was scared to death that I was going to get a cramp, which could have set us back several minutes. As it was we finished with no cramp, and it came just a few minutes after the race. So we were close, and I'd take the 4:01:05 time and hope that Chris pulled me into Boston.

We sent in the application and waited on needles and pins for months to hear from Boston. We finally got word that I got in. This April 2013, the 117th running of "the Boston," I will run again.

I feel like a prizefighter with another shot at the championship. My run at Boston five years ago at age sixty wasn't very good. In fact, it was the worst marathon time I ever had. Now I get to go back and have another shot at Boston.

I've had a lot of people ask me when I'm going to quit running, and I know what they're thinking—at your age maybe you ought to hang it up. I love what Jack Kirk said, "You don't stop running because you get old. You get old because you stop running."[1] As we grow older our bodies change partly because we're older but also because we do less physically. I want to keep going in my running, and I want keep going in my life.

I know the same question could be asked of my ministry—when will I retire? Jesus didn't say take up your cross and follow Me until age sixty-five and then take up your fishing pole. One may retire from a job but how do you retire from a calling? I haven't yet figured that out. I love my work as pastor, and I keep going. There are people yet to reach and vision still to accomplish.

We've lived our dream, and it has been a thrilling and exciting race. Gayle and I have often wondered what it would be like to be bored. Our lives are full and there is much to do. I tell our people the tomb is empty that our lives may be full. John 10:10 tells us, "He came that we may have life" and "have it more abundantly."[2] We are busy for Him and want to stay that way. He has blessed me with good health. In forty years of pastoring Calvary, I've never missed a Sunday because of sickness. As long as He continues that blessing, I want to be busy in His work with our team and our congregation.

In 2006 we began to think about expanding the worship center. The church was growing again and filling up, and we had been exhausting ourselves doing three services. I met with the deacons, and we had some preliminary studies done. One night we met for several hours talking and weighing our options. Every deacon was ready to go with the worship center expansion except one. One deacon hesitated and expressed his concern. He wasn't sure about the timing. The meeting went on, and we didn't have unanimity. Finally, one of the deacons said, "Well, Pastor, we're just going to leave it in your hands. You make the call. If you think we should proceed with building right now, then we're behind you."

I drove home from that meeting frustrated. I knew I would not go forward unless everyone was on board. This was a big step of faith. We were looking at a multi-million dollar project. We had a big task ahead of us. If I couldn't convince the deacons to be fully in support, how could I convince the entire church family?

We waited a whole year, and by 2007, because of continued growth, everybody was ready. We launched our Forward by Faith campaign, a three-year capital fundraiser, led by Jeff Ryan, who did a tremendous job.

While we were designing and planning the building, I made a lot of trips across town to meet with the architect and planning team. During one meeting with the architect, he said, "Pastor Carl, I have this idea. I thought about taking the steeple with the cross on top off of your first building and putting it over the entrance of the new building." For a minute I didn't say anything, and he looked at me and asked, "Is that a bad idea?"

I said, "No, I am just amazed you would suggest it. My dad made the cross on top of that steeple. Moving it from the first building to the new building is such a validation of the work and where we've come from."

Even though he was now gone, it gave me the chance to redeem a mistake I'd made with Dad early in the ministry. Way back when we built that first building, Dad, being a plumber, soldered copper pipe together to make that cross for the top of the steeple.

Shortly after that he said to me, "You don't like it, do you?" I was surprised and told him I had never said that. He was

Steeple with Dad's cross moved

abrupt, "Well, you didn't say you liked it." He was right. I hadn't acknowledged his contribution, but now I got to. It was a great feeling to put that cross onto the new building.

We started the Forward by Faith campaign, asking our people to make a commitment for three years over and above their regular tithes and offerings. Gayle and I talked and prayed about it and knew that, again, we needed to lead the congregation in our commitment. We sat down to look at our budget to see what we could give over three years. We came up with the cash amount we felt God would have us commit, but we felt that there was another opportunity to give back.

Over twenty years ago, God had provided our house in the country, while also providing for our children's college educations by allowing us to keep our house in the Highlands as a rental property. Through these two houses, He had given back our gift to the previous building campaign and more. Well, now that the kids were finished with school, we wanted to give the house in the Highlands back to God. We gave the deed to the church.

Likewise, our Calvary families prayed about their commitments and sought God's will. One after another they made sacrificial commitments by faith. God honored their faith, and I have heard story after story from our people about God's blessing in the midst of their giving.

We finished our building in 2009. Our first Sunday was Easter Sunday. A special excitement buzzed in the air that day. Over 1,700 people came to our three services. As I stood greeting people, I could see north out the glass walls of our new Connections Café lobby and fellowship area. People were parking and walking in, and traffic was backed up on First Street, around the corner, and down Superior Street.

Easter Sunday, 2009, first Sunday in new worship center

I was moved with emotion and made my way through the crowd to find a place I could be alone for a minute. I prayed and reminded God, "I'm in over my head. I'm a PK, a plumber's kid, and this whole thing was Your idea, not mine." A quiet calm filled me as I realized my confidence was in Him not me.

Little did I know just how much I would need that calmness. In the second service, the auditorium was packed as I started the Easter message, and something happened that had never happened in all my years of preaching. The fire alarm went off! It drowned out my voice and soon an automated voice came over the sound system telling people how to exit the building. I knew our new system was malfunctioning, and this was a false alarm. People seemed to sense that, too, and no one moved from their seats. I didn't want to lose anyone out of the service, and I knew if the firemen came, it would take a long time to check all the facilities, which could cancel the third service. So with the alarm still going off, I spoke as loudly as I could and asked everyone to just hold tight until our security team could shut off the alarm and let us know what was happening. Everyone remained calm and waited while our team got the alarm shut off and confirmed that all was well. No one slept through that sermon. They were wide awake.

Our children's team was on the ball, and the children had exited and were enjoying a fire drill when we let them know what had happened.

The most ironic thing about the alarm going off was just how it had happened. It was none other than our building superintendent, Mr. Fred Potts, who accidentally set it off. Fred was, in my opinion, a mechanical genius. He grew up in the Sandhills of western Nebraska in a house that was eight miles from the nearest road. When something broke out there, you didn't call a repairman; you fixed it yourself. Fred could fix anything. I often called him "Fix-it Fred."

I treasured his friendship, and he would often come out and help me on projects at my house out in the country. Time and again as we worked, he would tell me what Sunday's message meant to him. He always made me feel like I could out preach Billy Graham. When he retired, he came to work for Calvary, overseeing the church and school buildings on our thirty-six acre campus and, along with Galen Schweitzer, gave us many hours of faithful service.

With the great crowd that Easter morning, it got warm in church, so Fred went to our new system computer to override the programmed temperature controls and turn the air conditioner up but hit the wrong button and set the alarm off.

We were blessed to have Fred serve with us for ten years before God took him home. Now Sunday church isn't complete if I don't get a hug from his wife, Carolyn. I miss Fred, and when I see him in Glory, I'll still tease him about setting off the fire alarm.

Two months later, we dedicated our new building. Dr. Elmer Towns came and preached the dedication of that building just as he had for our other buildings and as he had preached our charter service years before.

Since we still owed on the building, we asked our people to go one more year. Forward by Faith had been three-year program, so we called the extra year's commitment Finish by Faith. Some of our people teased that we were heading for Forever by Faith. I didn't think that was a bad idea. What a great way to live—Forever by Faith. Our last year was better than any of the first three years. Our people gave enough that we were able to completely pay off the building.

We have served these forty years, and our goal is to continue to be faithful. We're not finished yet. There's another Boston to run. We have come through many dangers and toils and snares as "Amazing Grace" says, but we have experiences and challenges yet to come. We want to run the race with endurance as the Scripture says, and one day finish and have that great finish-line-feeling when our Lord says, "Well done, my good and faithful servant."[3]

AN UNEXPECTED TRAGEDY:
RUNNING MY SECOND BOSTON
APRIL 15, 2013

EPILOGUE

I hadn't planned to include the story of the 2013 Boston in this book. I had made that decision due in part to timing, the deadline was looming, and in part because I was happy with the last chapter looking forward to the upcoming Boston, the next race. I liked that you, the reader, would be left with a sense of ongoing possibility and future prospect. I wanted this book to be forward looking, always pushing on to the next dream.

But instead of being a day of dreams, April 15, 2013, turned out to be more like a nightmare. My experience that day was surreal, and I knew I couldn't end the book without addressing the stark realities that the Boston Marathon bombing brought into focus. This is the story of my experience that day. It is one story of thousands, many far graver than mine.

BOSTON, MASSACHUSETTES, April 15, 2013, Gayle drove me from our hotel in Framingham to the designated runners' drop off, which is a few miles from the start at Hopkinton. Before we said goodbye, I insisted on a kiss, and then Gayle surprised me by asking if she could pray for me. We don't typically pray together before a race, though I know she always prays for me as I run, but I didn't question her. We held hands, and she said, "God, give Carl's legs strength. Watch over him and keep him and take care of him today." Then I got out of the car and onto a school bus loaded with runners and spectators.

After the bus ride into Hopkinton, I walked with the crowd a mile to Athlete's Village where I waited an hour and a half for my starting wave to be called. There were acres of runners from all over the United States and many other countries. It was cold so, as runners often do, I pulled on a black trash bag I'd brought along for warmth while waiting. Like other runners, I spent most of my time in Athlete's Village in line to use a port-a-potty. I think they moved every port-a-potty east of the Mississippi there, but the lines were still long.

My wave, the third wave, was called, and I walked with all the other runners in my pace group the mile to Main Street, where we were herded into our starting corral. Soon we were off and running. As I crossed the starting line, I pushed the button on my GPS watch, which would tell me at a glance my pace time, total time, and distance.

The first time I ran Boston, I looked forward to participating in the honor and history of this marathon, and I wasn't disappointed. The day was weighty with importance, and I felt privileged to be a part of it. This time, I knew what to expect and was looking forward to soaking in the scenes and experiences of the day.

Day before Boston Marathon at Hopkinton, the start, as Carl and Gayle planned race strategy

In fact, I knew I'd have a little extra time to do that. I had planned before the race even started to run a slower than typical marathon pace due to over-training. Since I started long-distance running, I usually log 1,200 miles a year, but for 2012 I set a goal to run 1,500. I had reached that by November and decided to shoot for 1,800 instead. To make that goal, I averaged fifty-six miles a week for the last eight weeks of the year.

The first three months of 2013 were set aside as training for Boston. For my peak training run, Gayle and I drove to Oklahoma where I ran the Guymon Marathon that was part of the Dust Bowl Marathon Series. Of course, Guymon is Gayle's hometown. We enjoyed visiting her mother and her sister and husband, and they were a great curb crew for the race. As I ran that marathon, I noticed that I had a bad case of tired legs. A week later I tried to run ten miles at my typical marathon pace, nine-minute miles, and my legs turned to jelly around mile seven. It was clear I had over-trained.

I called both John and Chris for sympathy and advice. They both told me not to worry but to relax and have fun running Boston. Chris said, "This is your victory lap. Enjoy it."

I determined to hold back at Boston and planned to run ten-minute miles and then do my best to finish the last miles well. I knew this would probably be my last time to run this race, so my goal was to get the first twenty or so miles behind me, conquer the hills, and then enjoy the decline into downtown Boston. I wanted to immerse myself in the experience, take it slow, and have some steam left, so I could give it all I had when I saw mile-marker twenty-six and turned right on Hereford Street with my legs screaming but with cheering crowds pulling me through. Then I'd turn left on Boylston, see the finish up ahead, and enjoy that finish-line-feeling on the 117th running of the Boston Marathon.

I couldn't have imagined as I ran the first miles of the race and pictured the glorious finish that it would never happen. How could I know that instead of regretting my over-training and my inability to run my normal nine-minute pace, I would be thankful I was delayed? Who knew that this day, this perfect day, Patriots' Day, Marathon Monday, could be anything but glorious?

Gayle and I had outlined our race strategy the day before. We planned to meet at miles six and sixteen, where she would hand me a disposable bottle with my energy drink. Then, she wanted to hurry to Boylston Street to get a picture of me as I crossed the

Mile 6, Framingham

finish line. I wore a bright, greenish yellow shirt and ran on the north side of the street, so we could be sure to connect.

Just before mile sixteen, the Wellesley girls were a fun distraction. Each of them was holding a "Kiss-me" sign. "Kiss Me, I'm from Minnesota." "Kiss me, I'm an economics major." "Kiss me, I won't tell your wife." When I got to mile sixteen, I did get a kiss and another bottle of energy drink from Gayle.

I ran on thinking about Gayle. I knew she had to catch the train on into Boston and then walk several blocks to get to the north side of Boylston Street at the finish line as we had planned. Everything had to go right for her to make it there in time. I thought a prayer, "Lord, help her to make it, watch over her, and don't let my small town, Guymon girl get lost in this massive city." I had no idea that the last place I wanted her to be was the north side of Boylston Street at the finish line of the Boston Marathon.

Gayle hurried to the lot where she would park the car to take the train in. The lot was completely full, but she saw a family heading toward their car and waited impatiently for them to pull out. She's a get it done, task-oriented kind of person and is not famously patient. While she parked, she watched the train she had hoped to catch leave the stop. She waited anxiously for the next one, afraid she would miss my finish.

After seeing Gayle, I came to Newton and the four major hills, the fourth being Heartbreak Hill, which was everything I remembered it to be—brutal! At the top, I saw mile marker twenty-one and students from Boston College with their "Golden Mile" shirts and signs, letting us know it was all down hill into Boston now. The cheers of the crowd were deafening but welcome. The police were lined up to keep spectators back, but every now and then a student would duck under the tape and run with us for a hundred yards.

Their fun made our pain more bearable.

As planned I had saved enough energy to increase my pace for the last few miles of the race. That finish-line-feeling was ahead, and I still had some kick. I finally saw the big Citgo sign, which runners know as the landmark at the final mile. Now there was less than a mile to go until I would get my medal and give Gayle a sweaty hug.

Pushing to the Finish

But what was this? I could see runners up ahead, but they were not running. What was going on? Why were people stopped? We were so close to the finish.

Runners filled Beacon Street like bumper-to-bumper traffic—every one of them just standing there. I glanced down at my GPS, and the distance read 25.75. I was just a quarter mile from 26. Why were we stopped?

As I tried to make my way through the runners to see what was going on, three people ran back toward me. One lady ran into me spinning me sideways. Finally, someone with a cell phone told the crowd that a bomb had exploded at the finish. Another runner said he heard an explosion. I didn't hear the explosion, but the silence where the cheers of the crowd should have been was eerie.

Soon, a race official with a megaphone asked us to remain where we were because of an "incident" at the finish. He didn't tell us what had happened, but by now news had spread through the crowd that there had been an explosion. We did not know the magnitude of it. He called it an "incident." Maybe it was minor. That hope soon evaporated as emergency vehicles with sirens blaring rushed by one after another.

Race officials held us for nearly an hour. We were all wet with sweat and beginning to chill in the wind. One girl near me couldn't stop her teeth from chattering. Someone handed out black plastic trash bags to serve as jackets. I would wear mine for the next several hours.

Eventually, race officials informed us that the race would not continue. They directed us to walk out and around the finish area to get to the family meeting area.

I walked several blocks to the meeting area, but Gayle was nowhere to be seen. It was becoming obvious that this must have been a pretty big "incident." Police officers were everywhere. Emergency vehicles were speeding by to and from the finish line. Helicopters circled above us. The bomb squad moved in like an army with bomb-sniffing dogs.

As I walked around looking for Gayle, a reporter with the *Washington Post* asked me for an interview. He walked beside me asking questions. It dawned on me that I had no phone, no money. All I had was a trash bag and a Boston Finisher's wrap I had found and put on to keep warm.

David, the reporter, was so helpful. He pulled out his cell phone and tried to call Gayle, but cell calls weren't going through. We could not reach her. I didn't let myself think the worst. I wouldn't even let my mind go there.

Meanwhile, Gayle had boarded the next train and was just getting off in downtown Boston. She was hurrying through the station to get to the finish when police ran in and yelled, "Get out of this building now!"

Outside, Gayle was unsure what to do and had no idea why she had been rushed out. She decided to head toward the north side of Boylston Street to find me, still hoping she hadn't missed my finish. She asked someone, "Is the finish up this street?"

"Yes," he responded, "but you can't go there. The race is over. It's called off." People were standing in stunned disbelief not knowing what to do. Someone said a manhole had blown from a gas explosion, but another man came by who said, "A bomb has exploded. People are dead!" Of course, she soon saw scores of emergency vehicles and personnel.

At 3:03 she sent a text to our three kids, Carey, Carla, and Nathan: *Police rushed us out of subway station—runners have been stopped. Bomb threat or explosion of some kind. Runners have been stopped who had not finished. Sirens everywhere. Someone catch some news and let me know what is going on.* Before long they were able to tell her what the media were saying. The kids watching the news knew more than we did, really, and were very concerned. Nathan urged her to get out of downtown for fear there were more bombs. Then, due to lack of cell service, they lost touch with her. It would be over an hour before they would hear any first hand news of my whereabouts or reconnect with Gayle. They stayed on the phone together most of the afternoon, watching the news.

I felt so helpless. Sirens were blaring; people were running here and there. A lady stopped me and asked if I had seen a man with red hair, a runner about my height. I couldn't help her and saw the anxiety in her eyes as she continued her search.

David and I were still trying to call Gayle and having no luck. Gayle could see she was getting a call from a 202 area code, but the call dropped every time she tried to answer. She started walking away from the area near Boylston Street hoping to get better service.

We tried again and again and finally got through. I was so glad to hear her voice. We told her where we were and she headed to meet us.

David sat down to text his report to *The Washington Post*. Another reporter from the *Wall Street Journal* interviewed me, as well as a local T.V. station.

At last, I saw a more welcome sight than any finish line of any marathon—there was Gayle coming down other side of the street. I flagged her down so relieved to be together.

David walked several blocks with us to help us find a train station. As we walked, we passed a row of emergency vehicles, with lights flashing, backed up for blocks. Downtown felt upside down—both too quiet and buzzing with emergency noise at the same time. When we found a train that seemed to be running, we thanked David for his help.

In the station, Gayle found a bench and told me to sit a spell. She bought a large coffee to warm me up. As I sat there, a police officer went by with his bomb-sniffing dog. It seemed unreal, like something out of a T.V. show or movie or like a nightmare you can't escape. I couldn't do anything but sit and watch.

We rode the train west out of Boston. I looked out the window and felt numb. I called Carey, Carla, and Nathan and told them I love them—should do that more often. As I talked with them, what had happened began to register, though it still seemed like a bad dream—unreal. Here I was sitting on the train wearing a black trash bag. I had started the day in Athlete's Village keeping warm the same way. When I threw that trash bag away and headed toward the starting line, I was sure 26.2 miles later I would to cross the finish line and get my medal as I had in twenty-one previous marathons. Instead, I was riding a train out of Boston wearing another black trash bag, having never crossed the finish line. My first DNF.

I never thought I'd have DNF. As I've said throughout this book, I believe that persistence pays. I've always felt if I work hard enough, I will reach my goals. If I just keep running, I'll reach the finish line. But here I was, due to circumstances beyond my control and much bigger than me, with my first DNF.

In the introduction to this book, I talked about prayer and persistence adding up to faith. That equation takes into account both our part in the persisting and God's part in the praying to make our goals and dreams reality. The events of the 2013 Boston brought into sharp focus the prayer part of the faith equation. We can keep moving and keep persisting, until, well, we can't for reasons beyond us. Prayer does turn our persistence into substance, but perhaps more importantly, prayer can help us cope when persistence isn't enough and when things beyond our control happen.

Proverbs 27:1 says, "Do not boast about tomorrow, for you do not know what a day may bring forth."[1] The events of that day reminded me that those things we don't know and can't foresee—those things that are so unclear—move us toward the posture of prayer. It is prayer, really, that puts us in touch with that which is beyond us, with the unseen. In prayer we can ask for perspective and protection. It's easy to see the positives now in these things Gayle and I considered setbacks. Maybe when we can't run our best pace or we miss our train, we can be thankful. Openness to God's perspective can make all the difference. When we were stopped at 25.75 miles, my first reaction was anger. I ran all this way and couldn't finish? Then as I realized the real tragedy—lives lost, people hurt—no, no, how could this be? My loss was nothing. For some the day held not just a setback but unbearable grief. How does one deal with the fact that for some the day didn't hold a reunion like Gayle's and mine?

In one day I saw beauty and horror. The spring trees with white blossoms. The college kids having so much fun. Then the carnage and the fear. Those remarkable spectators who make the Boston finish spectacular were attacked. An eight-year-old boy ran out and hugged his daddy, who had just finished, and headed back to his mother and sister among the crowd to meet disaster. Over 200 people were injured, many severely. Three people were killed. How is it possible that these extremes exist in the same space and happen within such a short timespan?

Even my emotions in that day swung from elation at nearing the finish, to alarm at realizing what was happening, back to rejoicing at seeing Gayle, and then anguish over the devastation happening around me. Prayer is the response to both of these extremes. When we rejoice and when we grieve our hearts are pulled to prayer. And it is prayer that joins my experience of survival and reunion with the experiences of those for whom that day was utterly life altering. We all needed to touch what is beyond that day. It is prayer that allows us to do that, when we can rejoice and when we grieve.

It is this that drives me in ministry: God's power to change the hearts of people and His nearness in prayer. I am as committed as ever to walking with people through the joys and griefs that turn our eyes toward the power that is beyond us.

ACKNOWLEDGMENTS

I have found that writing a book is a lot like running a marathon. It is challenging, overwhelming, and after awhile you find yourself asking, "Whose idea was this, anyway?" I know this, when you have someone to run with you, the miles go by faster. "Two are better than one because they have a good return for their labor" Ecclesiastes 4:9 says.[1]

I owe a great debt of gratitude to my daughter Carla for being my companion in this marathon project. Who would have ever thought that the little kindergarten girl whom I assured that Jesus would take care of us would one day help me tell the story of how He did take care of us. Now she is part of God's provision because I know that I could not have done this without her. God has given Carla the gift of writing, and she has used her God-given gift and poured herself into this project. She took my boatload of stories and made sense of them for you. I am thankful to Carla for her work on the book and to God for Carla. I know He's used her and will continue to use her to further His cause in the future.

Yes, it's been work, but it's also been fun to run this race with you, Carla. Thanks!

Of course, I owe a big thank you to my Gayle. Like everything else in ministry in these forty three years of our marriage, you've been so helpful to me in the writing of this book. I know you spent hours scouring books to find my quotes since I just wrote them from memory. You read my scribbled notes and typed them out and have proofread each layer of our manuscript. You looked through archives, found pictures—as always picked up the loose ends.

Thanks for being my "curb crew" for this, another, different kind of marathon.

Jenny Smith of Smith Signature Design came in last minute to help us design and layout the cover and interior of *The Sermon Ran Long*. I don't know what we would have done without her. Her expertise and work ethic pushed this project through its final mile.

Next to my dad, no man has had a greater influence in my life than Dr. Elmer Towns. His book *The Ten Largest Sunday Schools And What Makes Them Grow* changed the very direction of my life. When I read that book, I never dreamed I would meet him let alone get to have him as a friend, mentor, and encourager. He believed in me and recognized potential I didn't know I had. I couldn't thank him enough for challenging me to follow my God-given dream.

Forty years ago he encouraged me to plant a church. More recently he encouraged me to write this book to give God the glory by telling the story. Once again his encouragement set me on a new journey for which I am deeply grateful.

To Chairman Todd Case and all the deacons who faithfully serve with me I owe a huge thank you. It was at your urging that I began this writing project. I couldn't do without your support and encouragement.

The pastoral staff at Calvary is a dream team, in my opinion. I am blessed to work with you. You stepped up and filled gaps while I focused on this project. I couldn't have made it the priority it needed to be without your help.

To the Calvary people I want to say a deeply felt thank you. You are the miracle of Calvary Community Church. You have believed God's promises and lived by faith. This story is about you, for you made it possible. I am deeply grateful for your encouragement and prayer for me through every step of this journey.

I love what we share at Calvary. It is special, rare, exciting, and joyful! Each week we come together to be with those we love and jointly express our love to Him who has done a miraculous work of grace in us.

To all who make up the Calvary family, you are "my joy and my crown, so stand firm in the Lord, my beloved."[2] Let's continue to live by faith so that we always have a story to tell for Him.

PIONEERS REMEMBERED

There are so many stories of people who have committed themselves to His cause at Calvary and whose lives have been changed by God's work. People who have stepped out by faith, trusting in His promises. You are the Calvary Faith Hall of Fame. I wanted to tell many more stories about what God has done through you but was reined in by those who had the responsibility of helping me with this project. They told me, "You've got to be realistic and narrow this down." I knew they were right; we couldn't go on forever. (Wait until we get home in Heaven.) So I say with the writer of the Faith Hall of Fame, "What more shall I say? For time will fail me if I tell of. ..."[1]

But persistent as always, I couldn't give up on telling a few stories. I proposed a section dedicated to a handful of people who came to Calvary Community Church during our years in rented buildings—our first four and a half years—and were foundational to the ministry that developed. I call them the Pioneers. Some of them have passed on, some have moved away, but there are a few who still serve with us. They have been faithful all these years and have been constants in my life and in the lives of so many who have come through our church. Whether or not they have often been recognized, their contributions to Calvary have been immeasurable in so many ways. I admire their persistent faithfulness and want to spend a few paragraphs acknowledging them.

When we were meeting in the Y building, **Russell and Ruby Sommers** visited our church. They were my parents' age. He was a very dignified looking, white-haired man and had been a school superintendent in the western part of the state.

They came for the first time to a Bible Study. There were only about twelve of us there. We sat around a table and studied the Bible and then spent some time in prayer. That night Gayle prayed and asked God's blessing on our ministry and called out to God. Sometime later Russell shared with me that when they heard Gayle pray, they decided this was the ministry they wanted to be involved in.

They would play such a significant role in the future of our church. While my dad was working in Alaska, Russell became a mentor to me. I relied on his advice. He became Calvary's first deacon chairman, and his wisdom was instrumental in shaping our church in the early years.

The Lord has taken Russell Home to be with Him. Ruby lives in Omaha near her children and grandchildren. We still keep in touch.

Dale Markussen and Russell Sommers lead deacons in breaking ground

Dale and Evelyn Markussen, another couple also about my parents' age, came to the church during those days at the Y building. Dale was a wiry guy. I don't think he weighed 140 pounds, but he was a tough cowboy. He had lived on a ranch most of his life. He had ridden in rodeos and always wore a western suit.

Dale used to love to go on visits with me. In those days, when somebody visited the church we would go to visit them at their home during the week. He liked to join me on my weekly visits, but in the winter, he insisted on driving. He didn't want to ride in my Volkswagen Beetle because those air-cooled engines didn't put out much heat at all, and you just froze. He was such an encouragement to me in those early years.

Dale has gone Home to be with his Lord, and Evelyn lives in Des Moines near her family.

One Sunday Dale and Evelyn brought their friends **Terry and Karen Boss.** I was so excited to meet them and wanted them to become a part of our church because they were good friends with Markussens.

Karen Boss and Evelyn Markussen

That week I went to visit Terry and Karen. I went to their apartment and knocked on the door. Terry opened the door about five inches, didn't even take the chain lock off, and said to me, "We're going back to our own church next Sunday." I thanked them for coming and walked back out into the night feeling discouraged.

Two Sundays later they were back. They said, "Well, we went back to our own church and realized we wanted to be here." Now, forty years later, Terry and Karen Boss are still actively involved. They serve as Prayer Partners, prepare meals for any occasions we host, and prepare Sunday morning refreshments and coffee in our Connections area. They are a great blessing to our church.

Terry and Karen Boss

During our third anniversary tent service, a man came forward at the close of the service inviting Jesus Christ to become his personal Savior.

The next day, a big brown Pontiac pulled in my driveway. The man who had come forward got out, came to my door, and said he wanted to visit with me. His name was Daymond. We drove to a nearby park and talked.

Daymond was bubbling over with enthusiasm. He said, "I gave my life to Jesus Christ yesterday." He went on, "I want you to come by, and I want you to tell that same message to my wife and my children. My wife's gonna get saved. My kids are going to get saved. I'm gonna get baptized. My wife's gonna get baptized, and my kids are going to get baptized. We're gonna be a part of building the church on that hill." Well, I thought maybe he was assuming too much of his family's interest in salvation and church, but that week I went by his house, and he was right. His wife and children did receive Jesus Christ, and they all got baptized in our church. Daymond had been a heavy drinker with a wild past, but his life was transformed. **Daymond and Cathy Francisco** were an important part of our church for years until the Lord took Daymond Home a few years ago. Cathy is still a greeter and dedicates herself to ministry in our church.

Francisco family dressed up for "old fashion day" at church

While we were meeting in the Belmont Community Center, somebody gave me the name and address of a family member they wanted to me to visit. I drove up to that address, knocked on the door, and told them who I was. They invited me in. I visited with **Don and Maxine Drevo** and began to share the gospel with them and tell them how they could know for sure that Jesus Christ was their personal Savior and Heaven was their eternal home. I told them we are all sinners and there's a penalty upon sin, but that Jesus Christ paid it for us. We can receive Him and receive the gift of eternal life. When I presented the gospel to Don and Maxine, they bowed their heads and each trusted Jesus Christ.

Don and Maxine Drevo

Don went from being a drinker to a deacon. He was a plumber and knew my dad. It had been a habit for him to close down bars. The church became his new bar and his new family. He became a Bible reader. He read his Bible through again and again. He reminded me of the grandfather in the story of *Heidi*: big, bearded, and gruff, but also, big-hearted, kind, and loving.

Every time we built a building, it seemed like Don got laid off from his job. He and Maxine would come over and work basically full-time. They always worked together. They were faithful Prayer Partners. We were blessed to have Don serve with us for thirty-seven years before God took him home in 2013. Maxine still serves as a Prayer Partner and is at church every week.

The week before our third anniversary tent service, I knocked on doors all over northwest Lincoln. One of those doors belonged to Mrs. Stanley. After we visited, she promised she would come on Sunday. When someone told me that, I didn't forget it. I wrote it down and prayed for her

Stanley family at Third Anniversary tent service

and her family and looked for her Sunday morning. She did come and brought her children. Her son Bill was in seventh grade at the time.

Bill Stanley has been faithful since that day. For thirty-seven years he has been a part of Calvary. He and his wife, Chris, serve as Prayer Partners, and he has helped with our audio and video equipment for years.

A quiet but committed couple came to Calvary in our first year as a church. Raymond and **Evelyn Holloway** were never up front folks, but they were always faithful behind the scenes. Evelyn worked in our nursery and rocked many babies who have grown up in our church. In

Evelyn Holloway in the nursery

my mind's eye, I can still see their smiles as they were seated among our little congregation in the Y building listening to me preaching His word.

Years ago they retired and moved to warm Florida, but their children Barb, Cheryl, and Dan are still part of our fellowship.

The contributions of these and countless other people built the work that is central to this story. Calvary Community Church is made up of some of the most committed people I've ever come across. I can't thank our congregation enough for their time and effort toward making Calvary what it is.

ENDNOTES

Introduction
1. KJV (Cambridge Edition).

Learning Persistence: My Early Years
1. Quoted in Scott Jurek with Steve Friedman, *Eat and Run: My Unlikely Journey to Ultramarathon Greatness* (Boston & New York: Houghton Mifflin Harcourt, 2012), 154.
2. Forrest A Dolgener, Tanjale Mabon Kole, and David A. Whitsett, *The Non-Runner's Marathon Trainer* (Chicago: Master's Press, 1998).
3. Dick Beardsley and Maureen Anderson, *Staying the Course: A Runner's Toughest Race* (Minneapolis & London: University of Minnesota Press, 2002), XI.
4. Quoted in Hal Higdon, *A Century of Running Boston: Celebrating the 100th Anniversary of the Boston Athletic Association Marathon* (Emmaus, PA: Rodale Press, 1995), 65.
5. NASB.

Realizing Potential Through Camaraderie: College Days
1. ESV.
2. II Corinthians 6:14a NKJV.
3. NASB.

More Than Like-To: Training for Ministry
1. Quoted in Dean Karnazes, *Run! 26.2 Stories of Blister and Bliss* (New York: Rodale Press, 2012), 40.
2. NASB.
3. NASB.
4. Elmer Towns, *The Ten Largest Sunday Schools and What Makes Them Grow* (Grand Rapids, MI: Baker Book House, 1970).

Walk With Wise Men: Forming Our Vision

1. http://www.leadership-with-you.com/john-wooden-leadership.html.
2. NASB.
3. NASB.
4. KJV (Cambridge Edition).
5. ESV.

He Who Began a Good Work: The First Years of Ministry

1. NLT.
2. NLT.
3. Philippians 1:6 NLT.
4. NASB.
5. NASB.

A Hero's Hug: Family Shapes Ministry

1. Quoted in *The Quotable Runner: Great moments of Wisdom, Inspiration, Wrongheadedness, and Humor* (New York; Breakaway Books, 1995, 2001) Editor Mark Will-Weber, 177.
2. I John 5:13 NASB.
3. Elmer Towns, *Getting a Church Started In the Face of Insurmountable Odds With Limited Resources In Unlikely Circumstances* (Nashville; Impact Books, 1975).

Unexpected Victory: Fighting for Religious Freedom

1. Dean Karnazes, *Ultra Marathon Man: Confessions of an All-Night Runner* (New York: Penguin, 2005), 235.
2. NASB.
3. NASB.
4. NKJV.
5. Dean Karnazes, *Ultra Marathon Man: Confessions of an All-Night Runner* (New York: Penguin, 2005), 231.
6. Names are changed to protect anonymity.
7. NKJV.
8. I Corinthians 15:57 NIV.

Surprising Sacrifice: God Provides in Unexpected Ways

1. NASB.

Run Through the Pain: Facing Internal Problems

1. Hal Higdon, *A Century of Running Boston: Celebrating the 100th Anniversary of the Boston Athletic Association Marathon* (Emmaus, PA: Rodale Press, 1995), 139.
2. Amby Burfoot, *The Runner's Guide to the Meaning of Life* (Eugene, OR: Daybreak, 2000), 115.
3. Name is changed to protect anonymity.
4. Name is changed to protect anonymity.
5. NASB.

Iron Sharpens Iron: Building Our Team

1. NIV.
2. NIV.
3. Matthew 16:18 NLT.

Still Running the Race: The Church Endures

1. Quoted in Christopher McDougall, *Born to Run: A Hidden Tribe, Superathletes, and the Greatest Race the World Has Never Seen* (New York: Vintage, 2009), 202.
2. NASB.
3. Matthew 25:23 NLT.

Epilogue

1. NASB.

Acknowledgements

1. NASB.
2. Philippians 4:1 NASB.

Pioneers Remembered

1. Hebrews 11:32a NASB.

MEET **CARL GODWIN**

Carl Godwin is the founding pastor of Calvary Community Church, where he has served for forty years. Having accepted Christ as his personal Savior as a child, Carl felt God's calling to the pastorate at the age of sixteen.

Following graduation from Lincoln High School, he received his B.A. and M.A. degrees. In 1995 he was awarded an honorary doctorate degree from Liberty University.

Carl and his wife, Gayle, met during college and have been married over forty years. Following graduation, they set out on a journey to observe some of America's fastest-growing churches. During this time, they both began to sense God's leading to begin a church in Carl's hometown, Lincoln, Nebraska. That church became Calvary Community Church.

Carl and Gayle have three children and eleven grandchildren. Want to get Carl talking? Ask him about his dog Scout or his current marathon training.

Carl can be reached at cgodwin@mycalvary.org or at Calvary's website mycalvary.org.

MEET **CARLA EWERT**

Carla Ewert is a freelance writer and editor. Her editing experience ranges from web content to short stories. She has taught college level writing and is a blog contributor. She holds bachelors' degrees in Sociology and Bible from Grace University in Omaha, Nebraska, and a master's degree in English from the University of Nebraska at Omaha.

She lives in Minneapolis, Minnesota, with her husband, Chris, and daughter, Alice. They are expecting an addition to the family in August of 2013.

On a nice day in the Twin Cities, Carla enjoys cycling on the city trails or playing at Lake Harriet with her family. The long northern winters give her plenty of time for her other hobbies—hot coffee and good books.

Carla can be reached at carlae.12@gmail.com.

Photograph by Michelle Hepburn